THE REVIEW *of* CONTEMPORARY FICTION

ROBERTO CALASSO ISSUE

FALL 2015

VOL. XXXV, NO. 3

PUBLISHER

JOHN O'BRIEN

EDITOR

ALEX ANDRIESSE

PRODUCTION

KIRBY GANN

REVIEW OF CONTEMPORARY FICTION
Fall 2015
Vol XXXV, No. 3

The *Review of Contemporary Fiction* is published three times each year (January, June, September). Subscription prices are as follows:

Single volume (three issues):
Individuals $17.00 US; $22.60 Canada; $32.60 all other countries
Institutions: $26.00 US; $31.60 Canada; $41.60 all other countries

ISSN: 0276-0045
ISBN: 978-1-62897-333-4

Indexed in *Humanities International Complete, International Bibliography of Periodical Literature, International Bibliography of Book Reviews, MLA Bibliography, and Books Reviews Index. Abstracted in Abstracts of English Studies.*

The *Review of Contemporary Fiction* is also available on 16mm microfilm, 35mm microfilm, and 105mm microfiche from University Microfilms International, 300 North Zeeb Road, Ann Arbor, MI 49106-1346.

Cover photograph: *New York* by Arthur Holitscher, from *Amerika: Heute und Morgen* (Berlin: S. Fischer Verlag, 1923).

Address all correspondence to:
6271 E 535 North Road
McLean, IL 61754

www.dalkeyarchive.com

CONTENTS

THE REVIEW *of* CONTEMPORARY FICTION

ROBERTO CALASSO

AMERICAN HALLUCINATIONS

If there is a novel that allows us to understand what cinema is, it is *The Man Who Disappeared*. Karl Rossmann's eye is already the lens of the movie camera—and the America presented to him is a hallucinatory vision of everything cinema has become to date.

Cinema, for its part, is consubstantial with hallucination (figures in motion shifting on a cloth screen, like mental images on the backdrop of the mind) and with physicality (the bodies of the actors and actresses perceived with a sense of intimacy that lies at the origin of the fetishistic cult of the star). It is above all then a new—and highly paradoxical—mode of entering into contact with simulacra, if this word is taken to signify something that incorporates all the potentialities of images. Cinema means, above all, the co-presence of hallucination and hyper-reality, understood to mean *excessive* physicality. Now, if there is a novel where that deviant and extremely strange mode of perception is presented on the page, it is precisely *The Man Who Disappeared*. Why? It is not easy to say, and would require a microscopist, step-by-step examination. But it is a strong impression, which the reader cannot shake. This also explains why the book is so distinctive, even though the events it relates, after all, might be found in any naturalistic novel, à la Dreiser, about the misadventures of a young emigrant.

The very concept of the cinema hall and the cinematic spectacle tend to reconstruct the condition of a mind, in isolation, intent on hallucinating. This helps us understand why the spectator's sole ceremonial activity consists in eating popcorn. It is the gesture that forces the eye to remember it belongs to a body. The ritual of the theater or the concert is completely different, as an old essay by Adorno, "The Natural History of the Theater," admirably demonstrated. There, the darkness is not total, the spectators recognize and acknowledge each other (not like at the cinema, where it is essential they ignore each other: the moment of intermission is terrible, because it forces the cinemagoer to realize that there are people around him), and finally—this is the crucial passage of the rite—there is applause.

For all these characteristics, cinema is a metaphysical material par excellence. The spectator goes into a movie house as in the nineteenth century one went into—shall we say—a *rêverie*. The ideal spectator is the one led into the theater after the film has begun. (And it is quite perfect that, more often than not, it has been a woman who guides him—and that this woman has been called a *maschera*.[1]) Deviating a few meters from the street, where *normal* life unfolds, the spectator goes into a place of darkness, where images are set loose on a milky backdrop. Nothing is more like going into a *rêverie*. Here, too, there is no clearly defined starting point. There is a swerve away, a deviation (however minimal it may seem) from the trajectory of waking life. And immediately you enter a realm unknown to those who continue to pass by, busy and functional, on the street outside the cinema. Karl Rossmann's arrival in New York is like that swerve away, that deviation, which leads into a place there will be no escaping.

---

1. Literally, "a mask" or "a façade." [Editor's note]

Arthur Holitscher published *Amerika* in 1912, the year in which, on September 26, Kafka began the first draft of *The Man Who Disappeared*. After his death, Max Brod would give the novel the title *Amerika*. The book by Holitscher, a vigorous reporter, intended to provide a picture of America "today and tomorrow" (this was the subtitle) and from end to end. The opening scene could not but be the transatlantic liner from which, one morning, New York would loom in the mist. One day, sitting on the deck beside the other passengers—the canonical situation for getting acquainted on a voyage—Holitscher had found himself sitting next to a "distinguished" American, a sailor who had just won a race at Kiel and even met Wilhelm II. What had they talked about? "The emperor asked him how good society in America deals with rich Jews," and the sailor "gave him an answer." We do not know what it was. Holitscher had introduced himself by saying: "I want to go and see how America treats poor people." The sailor had answered by advising him to go to Newport, where the rich are. He would never get an all-around image of America "if he didn't see the smart set dancing in Newport."

Last dinner aboard. Women show off their best makeup and pierce their hair with tiny little umbrellas made of Japanese paper. The sailors say: "No one goes to sleep tonight." In the morning, hot humid air. The "gigantic wheel" of Coney Island appears. And finally the Statue of Liberty, "with the sun on the green folds of her dress and her foot resting on Liberty Island." But there is something else, too: "Just behind, some wide low red buildings, half lazaretto, half prison." What's that? asks Holitscher. They answer: "Ellis Island, the terrible island of emigrants." Meanwhile, Manhattan is drawing nearer "like a hand, long and narrow, thrusting upward, and you do not know: is it a greeting or a threat?

Kafka used Holitscher's book as a guide, not only for the text but for the photographs that illustrated it, while writing *The Man Who Disappeared*. Where one of the most disconcerting images occurs at the start. The Statue of Liberty does not brandish a torch, but a sword. This was not a slip, but a mark imprinted on the whole book. And Holitscher's reportage provided the background for that searing image, which stood at the threshold of the novel and foretold it all.

That New York is the place where you don't look so much as you are looked at by innumerable eyes, which open and close with the lights of the buildings, is an intuition that underpins the whole of *The Man Who Disappeared*. Karl Rossmann moves like a fairytale hero in search of adventures, but he is treated from the first *by everyone* as a guinea pig, both when he is impeccably cared for and when he is knocked around. Karl is a test animal—a *sacrificial* animal, as they say in the lingo of the lab. At first he is nurtured and protected in every way, as long as he lives with his uncle in New York. Then brusque and brutal treatment winds up prevailing. From this comes the pathos of the book, which is at once archaic and cruelly modern, with a modernity that has not yet been perceived. And Karl is an admirable character because he always maintains both the élan of the fairytale hero and the foggy perspective of the progressive degradation into which he is forced.

Kafka seems to have somnabulistically pursued, throughout his writing life, what was for him a preexisting novelistic structure, which revealed itself to him little by little: the story of an individual who is called or thrown into a world that there is no escaping. Karl Rossmann is deported to America. K. considers himself called to the Castle. But their vicissitudes are parallel and counterpointed, along with those of Josef K., who is summoned, then swallowed up, by the court. There is always an intervention from the outside, which sets everything in motion—and there is always an unknown territory that the individual will have to tread and explore. America, for Karl Rossmann, was this territory. And he entered it, unable to escape, as though wandering on the surface of a film.

With *The Man Who Disappeared*, Kafka intended to write the novel of "ultra-modern" New York (as he himself said). Therefore he was dismayed when Kurt Wolff, great publisher though he was, used for the cover of *The Stoker* (the beginning of the novel and the only part that Kafka himself published) an innocuous cartoon that seemed rather to refer to some Baltic port or other, and was irremediably nineteenth century. Kafka was thinking instead of something that would be understood at once, if you were leafing through photo books of New York in those years, like *Greater New York Illustrated*, which is from 1901. Here the pre-skyscrapers show themselves in all their imposing strangeness. They look like armor-plated animals, dropped there by the sky rather than grown from the earth. And they dominate the buildings around them as if they belonged to another level of reality. It is this, we may suppose, that attracted Kafka. Even to the letter. In one of these images, of the St. James Building on Broadway, one readily sees something of the rich uncle's building, where Karl Rossmann spends his first weeks in New York.

One of the photographs in Holitscher's book is emblematic of the America of *The Man Who Disappeared*. At the center, in the night, a dazzling skyscraper: a high tower on which there is a flag fluttering. It's unclear what could be the source of so much light, which isolates the outline of the building. Next to it is another skyscraper, but dark, except for four lighted windows. And the photograph wouldn't permit us to grasp how high this second skyscraper soars, if it were not for a faint light projected on the sky, perhaps from its roof. Around and below the dazzling tower, the buildings are solid darkness, as if they served only to accentuate the luminous part. But lower down there are three patches of light. They are as many streets. Then there is life, somewhere. But the lights seem disconnected, inexplicable. The center of the image is pure blackness.

The originary cell of Kafka's three novels, if considered as a whole, dates back to his years at Gymnasium: "Once I planned a novel in which two brothers fought each other, and one went to America, while the other remained in a European prison."

One summer Sunday, Kafka found himself with his family, visiting his grandparents. He also remembered, of that day, an especially soft kind of bread they smeared with butter. Meanwhile he'd started writing "something about my prison." Perhaps "out of vanity," he added, he did it all to make someone curious enough to take the page from him, read it, and admire it. But what was he writing about? "In those few lines the main thing described was the prison corridor, above all its silence and coldness." Finally an uncle "who loved to laugh" picked up the page: "He looked at it briefly, handed it back to me without laughing, and only said to the others, who were following him with their eyes: 'The usual stuff.'" And said nothing to Kafka, who then remembered: "I remained seated and bent as before over my now useless page, but in fact with that single thrust I had been cast out of society, my uncle's judgment kept repeating in me with what amounted almost to real significance and, even within the feeling of family belonging, a vision of the cold space of our world opened before me, which I had to warm with a fire that I first had to seek myself."

Kafka jotted down these words in his *Diary* a few months before he started writing *The Man Who Disappeared*. A novel "splashed all across the sky," and like the sky borderless, but written proceeding from the corridor of a prison. This was his America.

Translated from the Italian by Alex Andriesse

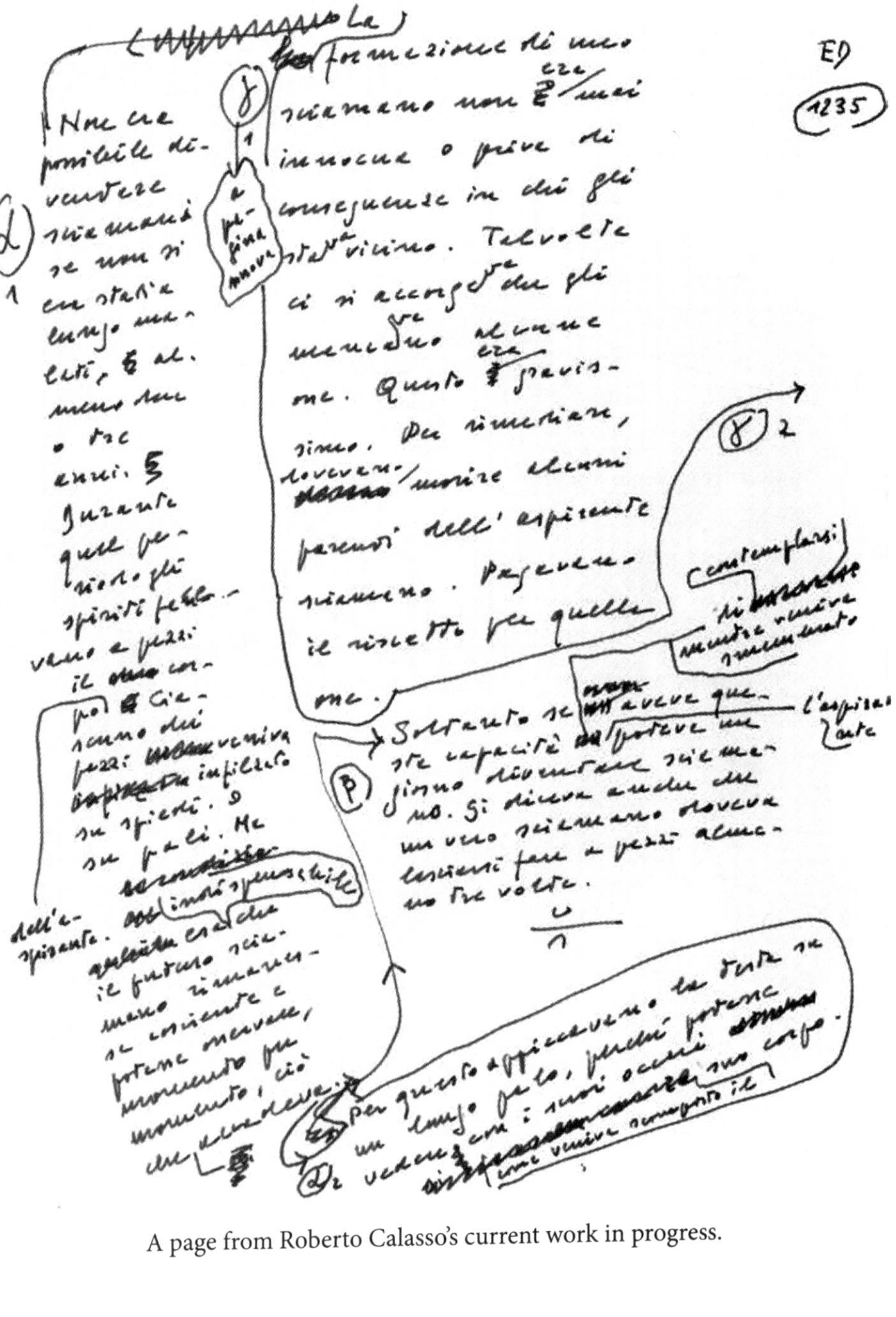

A page from Roberto Calasso's current work in progress.

ROBERTO CALASSO AND ALEX ANDRIESSE

A CONVERSATION WITH ROBERTO CALASSO

This conversation took place on the afternoon of June 7, 2018, in Roberto Calasso's office at Adelphi in Milan.

ALEX ANDRIESSE: I wanted to begin by asking how you see the different volumes of your Work in Progress in relation to each other. In particular, how do you see the books about historical European subjects (*The Ruin of Kasch, K.,* *Tiepolo Pink, La Folie Baudelaire*) in relation to the mythological books (*The Marriage of Cadmus and Harmony, Ka, Ardor*)?

ROBERTO CALASSO: Let's start from the beginning. *The Ruin of Kasch* is apparently totally history, but the first lines are already a Vedic myth, after all, and myths are intertwined throughout the book. Moreover, the simple art of telling a story is at the center, because Far-li-mas is the protagonist of the legend of the Ruin of Kasch, which itself is a sort of primordial myth, although it is known only in that version that Frobenius wrote down. What changes in every book is the texture of style. As everyone can see, *The Ruin of Kasch* is a highly hybrid form, where you have all sorts of literary genres mixed: you have letters, you have fragments and aphorisms, theoretical digressions, you even have two poems and a theater scene. And that corresponds to the central matter of the book, which is what is called "modernity." Now modernity itself is defined by this mixture of elements. On the other hand, you read *Ka,* for example, and *Ka* goes straight from beginning to end through what is really a tangle of Indian stories, and of course the stories are always mixed with reflections, with thoughts, with elaborations of concepts; but that is the physiology of our mind, I think. It's not a special invention. And so each book

has a different kind of style and form. But the two elements you were asking about—myth and history—are present everywhere. That doesn't happen, of course, in the book on Kafka, because Kafka means a sort of self-sufficient world where one gets in and doesn't want to get out. Though everything is reflected in that world.

AA: And the narrator of the Work. Do you think of him as being the same throughout? One sees certain metaphors and certain motifs wonderfully reappearing from book to book.

RC: The ideal thing would be that the narrator may be totally invisible. That's what my highest aim would be, and I don't know if I've managed it. But I write as if he was invisible. The things should speak for themselves, in some way. Well, after all, myths used to speak for themselves since forever. I don't need a special voice, but a plurality of voices. I know that some of these books are in a way terribly personal, like *La Folie Baudelaire* or *Tiepolo Pink*, but I think the same applies there, because after all they're definitely not history of art, they're definitely not history of literature. They're literature, simply, and literature is something which happens in front of one and doesn't need to be something else. I think it would be a big mistake if all this was connected too easily to what is supposed to be the psychology, or whatever else, of the author. That doesn't mean that the books are not terribly, even obsessively, linked one with the other. I think that must be totally clear now after so many years, with nine books. Sometimes I think that these connections are almost too evident. And they may be a surprise for me too. For instance, in that interview I sent you, done by Jaubert when *The Ruin of Kasch* was published in France: it was even a surprise to me to see that certain expressions which appear in *The Unnamable Present*, for instance "the superstition of society," are already there. It was already very clearly defined there. And that was '86. So a long time ago. Even "absolute literature," which is something I dealt with particularly in *Literature and the Gods*, is there throughout *The Ruin of Kasch*. So in a way I think I can be accused of all sorts of things, except that I'm not stubborn and I don't follow very constantly a certain line. Even more so because when I did that interview I was writing *The Marriage of Cadmus and Harmony*, but I had no idea, even in that moment, that after *The Marriage* there would be *Ka*.

AA: You've said before you had no plan to write a book about the Vedas. How did *Ka* come about?

RC: After *The Marriage of Cadmus* it was, in a way, like passing from a forest to a jungle. Only that Indian jungle is comparable to the forest of Greek myths. And I had to do with Indian things all the time, since before *The Ruin of Kasch*. They have always been essential to me. But I hadn't ever dealt with this huge proliferation of stories, which is Indian myth. So *Ka* was a surprise. And, when I was writing *Ka*, I was not thinking at all that the following book would be a book on Kafka, which was like going from the maximum proliferation to the maximum reduction. That was because Kafka doesn't pardon you if you expand too much. It's a big misunderstanding if you do that. You must keep sort of playing with very spare elements, and that's what I tried to do. So it was the opposite. And at the same time the two books were closely linked for one reason, which is explicit in *Ka*, and you find it in two lines where I say that Prajapati, the progenitor of all the gods, has a relation to the gods similar to that of the K. of Kafka to the characters of Balzac and Dickens. K. in a way tries to show that—and at the same time it does something which was very disconcerting for the legion of interpreters of Kafka, which is that I established some connections to some Vedic categories, with which Kafka had no relation at all. But it doesn't matter. The relation is in the things. Then there were special cases like *La Folie Baudelaire* and *Tiepolo Pink*. *Tiepolo* was initially a part of *La Folie Baudelaire*. And then it was cut out of it like a branch from a tree. The trunk was *La Folie Baudelaire*. So I concentrated on Tiepolo and it appeared first, but in fact I see both Tiepolo and Baudelaire as two ways of looking at *le peintre de la vie moderne*, that's to say at modernity itself.

AA: In fact *The Unnamable Present* seems to have grown out of the last section of *Ardor* and, more particularly, out of *The Ruin of Kasch*.

RC: In a way, it's a similar case to what happened with *Ka* in relation to the two lines on Prajapati. "The unnamable present" are three words isolated in *The Ruin of Kasch*. And in fact in the beginning the idea for me was to write not nine or more books, or whatever—I don't know in fact how many—but to write three: two were *The Ruin of Kasch* and *The Marriage of Cadmus and Harmony*, and the third one would be a short book about what is around us. And so it happened, but many years later, with *The Unnamable Present*. I postponed the book for thirty years. I will tell you how it happened. A year and a half ago, I was planning to put together some essays or articles I had published, but never put together in a book. And then some of them, I realized, had to be part of something else, and that was a part which started as a speech that I gave in Paris and then at Stanford, which is more or less at the beginning of *The Unnamable Present* now. And then it developed in this form. And the second part was something that I had written already in large part years ago and waited for something else where it would fit. So you see it was a surprise first of all to myself. It was not planned as it happened. If I plan something, it's sure that I won't do it exactly as I had planned. That I can say.

AA: In the English world at least, your books are often talked about as being written in a "new form." Is that fair to say?

RC: As to form, the most disconcerting and anomalous book in my ongoing work might be *The Celestial Hunter*. There you have fourteen parts and each has a totally different setting. One is an exploration of deep prehistory, focused on the passage of man from prey to predator, so its temporal range is huge. And another one is about a single night—the so called "night of the Hermocopids"—in Athens in the fifth century BC. Two other parts are straight narratives, mythical stories. Another one is set in Egypt. Another one is on the goddess Artemis. And there is a part on Plato's *Laws* and one on Plotinus. Still, a good reader may easily understand—I believe—how all these different sections converge on the same subject, which is what the Greeks called *to theîon*, "the divine." And on metamorphosis, with a range of material going from Inuit shamans to Turing. So I might say that in *The Celestial Hunter* I tried to do something which may appear outrageous to many. I was trying to show that Homo the Scavenger and Plotinus belonged to the same overall figure and should not be considered separately from each other, as paleoanthropologists and scholars of Plotinus usually do.

AA: In the other books, too, there's hardly anything formally comparable in recent English writing. Geoff Dyer may be the only Anglophone writer I can think of whose books consistently incorporate other books and remain literature, without becoming scholarship.

RC: His books have no genre, no clear genre—and that's why there's an affinity, in a way. He said to me once, you want to plunge immediately into the subject, and yes, that's absolutely true. So all these books should, from the first line, be *inside* the subject, totally. No preliminaries. And that, of course, can be disconcerting—especially, you know, if you think that Vedic India is not exactly the India travelers come across today. But that's why, I think, *Ka* and *Ardor* were received so warmly in India by so many who felt they were discovering, through these books, parts of their past they knew only vaguely about. I noticed that, even among cultivated people, if they knew the Upanishads, still they generally ignored the Brahmanas, to which the Upanishads belong. But this way of plunging into the subject applies even to *Tiepolo*. And even *Tiepolo* certainly doesn't follow the rules of the historians of art.

AA: To have an introduction in one of these books—at least an introduction in the scholarly sense—would really take something away.

RC: Absolutely. They should appear abruptly. Which may be shocking, sometimes. Some people might prefer to go somewhere else, but others will plunge in, and they go on. For certain readers, it was obvious from the beginning. Brodsky was the reader who saw it most immediately. But I think this same thing in fact applies to all these nine books, whether they are mainly narrative or mainly something else.

AA: I've just typed up the Brodsky piece, which is remarkable, and then there's the Calvino piece as well . . .

RC: Brodsky is the only one who seems to speak from the center of the book. But Calvino as well is excellent. *The Ruin of Kasch* was a book which struck him deeply. After the piece appeared, we talked about it a lot. In his last years, Calvino was circling around certain of these things and getting away from lots of things he had been involved in for a long time—and in a way going against himself, as he knew he would. Dangerous ground. But his reaction was terribly lucid.

AA: I think you quote just one little line of that review in *The Unnamable Present*.

RC: Which one?

AA: About the abolition of the gods' dwelling-place ranging from . . .

RC: From the end of the Paleolithic to the beginnings of the Industrial Revolution. Absolutely. But I didn't want to say, "in a review of one of my books..." He was very witty there. If one wants to find a sort of word around which everything turns, you can find it even before *The Ruin of Kasch*, because I realized myself a posteriori that *The Impure Fool*, my novel of 1974, was in fact a sort of prelude—a prelude in heaven or hell—but anyway a prelude to all the books of my work in progress. And that novel starts with the sort of breach in the order of the world which happens in the times of the ancestors of President Schreber, in Prussia. But in fact it's all about *rta*, that Vedic word which means at the same time "order of the world" and "truth". And that word appears in the beginning of *The Ruin of Kasch*. So the various metamorphoses of the order of the world are, I think, something which you find in all these books. And it's an endless task, in a way, because you never know where you get and from where you start. And then you get to today, when these words have a totally different meaning. In *The Unnamable Present*, I mention a book by Kissinger on "world order," thinking of the balance of powers, because simply the other meaning is totally forgotten. Today, if one says "world order," it's a question of what Russians can do versus the United States or China or vice versa. It's a proof in fact of what I call the superstition of society: nobody dares to go beyond that sort of horizon. It's strange. What is strange is that it is taken for granted. That it seems to be obvious if things are like that. But if you think of, not only India, but even Greece, the cosmos was something else from the polis.

AA: Kafka would seem to be one of the modern writers you identify as being highly conscious that there *is* something beyond society.

RC: Kafka, for every possible reason, is something apart. You have to change your lexicon when you come to him, and if possible keep as near as you can to the letter, to what he says, without adding other things. But I have to say he is the writer to whom I refer in my mind most often, because for him it was absolutely natural to see things in this way, which went beyond whatever society could imagine—beyond whatever he had around him. And that applies, I would say, totally to him, but I couldn't think of many other examples. Though of course there are great writers, for instance Proust—who for me is most important—who are apparently totally immersed in a certain social world, but at the same time go so much beyond that even they belong to the same tribe.

AA: In *The Ruin of Kasch* especially, it's clear the narrative is steering clear of the usual sort of sociological approach to history. There's an attempt, it seems to me, to look at society both from within and without.

RC: In that interview with Jaubert, I have a formula which I think applies very well to the book. Not only to that book, but to other things, and that I have used only there, which is the following: an anamorphotic vision of time, so applying anamorphosis, a distortion, in time rather than in space. That is essential for *The Ruin of Kasch*. This fact of things being at the same time very far apart and simultaneous. So, if you change the angle, you have Pol Pot coming immediately after Talleyrand or the Vedas. And that is something useful to define the way in which the book is made, because it is the opposite of the usual linear view of history, going either always toward what is better or what is worse. It's the same, after all. And that is totally alien to me.

AA: On the subject of sacrifice, you say in the Jaubert interview: "The error, the danger, is the solution. It's thinking that everything can have a solution." You've now examined the subject of sacrifice in the Vedas and the Greek myths, as well as in the French Revolution and in twenty-first century terrorist attacks. Is it such a potent subject in part because it is a problem without a solution?

RC: Solution is a very important word. But not for me. Especially in the Anglo-American or Scandinavian world, lots of people think they are very practical and they want whatever you say to have a solution. And, unfortunately, I have very bad news on that point, because I think it's the main social democratic mistake to think that everything has a solution. "Just give us enough time": that is the social democratic way of thinking. Well, being in Holland you have an experience of that. The secular, enlightened people are open to whatever you can think or whatever you can imagine, they are full of generosity and open to all sort of things, and they say, "Well, just wait a little, we have science, we have technology, we'll go step by step toward the end of the way and find the solution," except that it doesn't work, or at least, it works for many things—terribly impressive—but fundamentally minor. The essential things are things that—well, you started with the word *sacrifice*. Imagine someone telling you "I have the solution for what sacrifice is." It would be ridiculous. It's something really almost offensive. Or death. Well, some people are convinced of that, particularly today. "Just wait a moment, we are implementing a few things." And death might be a prejudice, in a way. No, I'm afraid not. In that same interview, I mention Flaubert on *la rage de vouloir conclure* being the worst thing. And that's why I'm writing the tenth volume—because I don't even imagine getting to any type of conclusion. Because there is no conclusion. The best you can do is to go from one point to another and then back, and then you start again, and then go in another direction; all the rest seems to me a naïve—and maybe a noble—illusion. With the best honed arguments they want to find solutions, and when this way of thinking applies itself to society it's even more disastrous, because all the twentieth century was more or less guided by people who were offering solutions. One should remember that. In Germany and in Russia as well. And it applies, too, to the most enlightened democratic societies. They follow more or less a line where, in the end, one by one, you may put things in order. But there is a final disorder of everything, which you cannot heal so easily. And so that is a point. And that applies to all my books. And that's why sacrifice reappears in all these books. Because I realized after a while it is in fact one of the most difficult things you can think of. And it's really inexhaustible. The idea of having come to fully understand certain phenomena is highly doubtful. After all you deal, in sacrifice, with a very strange form, which is rather absurd, because why should people, for instance, kill animals in order to appease or to make something appreciated by an invisible entity? And this gesture starts off very early and appears practically everywhere, so one should be very careful when one tries to understand it. One should change angles many times.

AA: Because your work is literature and not literary criticism or history or something well defined, solutions in the usual sense would be out of the question. But you don't have a sort of master plan?

RC: Not at all. It happens that at certain moments I feel that I have to tackle certain things. As to Kafka, for instance, I had in mind since I was more or less twenty that some day I should write something on him but it took a long time and even the book I'm writing now I have postponed for many, many years. But at a certain moment how does everything begin? It begins just by writing. And that's something I did since I was a young man and without any special sort of aim. At a certain moment certain things took a certain shape, and so it happened with *The Ruin of Kasch* as for *The Marriage of Cadmus and Harmony*. And there's a case which was a sort of a paradigm for all of this, *The Impure Fool*. I wanted to publish the memoirs of Schreber with Adelphi and the memoirs needed a sort of introduction just to explain what was this strange book of which I had revised the translation. The time came when I should write the introduction and then I realized that I couldn't. That it was a delirium to which I could respond only with another delirium. And I wrote in a very short time—I think a few weeks—that novel, after which I wrote—I finally wrote—an essay, not on Schreber but on the readers of Schreber. It is published in *The Forty-Nine Steps*. So you see how things start and every time it is a surprise, in a way. That was a very typical moment.

AA: You find the form just by continuing to write.

RC: Yes, that's it. Absolutely. I always keep a notebook in my pocket and in a way I cannot say I write only in the morning or afternoon or night, as some people do. It can happen at any moment. And so it was with *The Ruin of Kasch*. Except that for certain things from the beginning you have a sort of feeling of the dimension of the whole. You know, Karl Kraus made once a beautiful observation; he said that the first sentence of something implies the whole. So the first sentence of a book of five hundred pages implies the five hundred pages. Or if it is a sonnet, it implies a sonnet. And so I felt in certain moments that I was starting something which would be rather long or not long or whatever, and for instance for *The Unnamable Present* I felt the opposite—that it should be short. And I don't know why. I don't know exactly why. But that it should be sort of compact and dense.

AA: That book ends with that very eerie passage by Baudelaire, about the tower.

RC: I was of course tempted to put that passage in *La Folie Baudelaire*, but it didn't belong there, it was waiting for another moment. It's strange. I didn't know why myself. But it happened. I think it's right as it is.

ITALO CALVINO

ROBERTO CALASSO, *THE RUIN OF KASCH*[1]

The Ruin of Kasch takes up two subjects: the first is Talleyrand, and the second is everything else. And by everything else I mean what has happened in the history of humanity from the beginnings of civilization to the present day. This bipartition may seem a bit unbalanced, but it must be acknowledged that if ever a single person did all he could to encompass in himself a compendium of universal history, it was this French ex-prelate and diplomat, who was first a bishop under Louis XVI, then a deputy to the Constituent Assembly during the Revolution, then Napoleon's Minister of Foreign Affairs, then Louis XVIII's right-hand man during the Restoration, and who stayed in the saddle with Louis-Philippe after the July Revolution. The prototype of the turncoat, of the cynic who thinks only in terms of power and embodies power's commitment to perpetuate itself at any cost, Maurice de Talleyrand has always gotten what you might call bad press among historians. Roberto Calasso, on the other hand, spins a paradoxical apology for him. Why?

Because in the face of the cataclysm to which he is a witness (and an interested party)—that cataclysm which Calasso sees not only as the end of the Ancien Régime, but as the end of the cyclical, ritual, sacrificial world, replaced by raison d'état, social experiments, political processes, and mass carnage— Talleyrand understands that the only possible response is to operate under conventions without believing in them, thereby transforming tragedy into its opposite: the salon, the idle conversation, the masquerade, with all their political correlatives: intrigue, ceremony as a mask of reality or of nullity, declarations of principles as justification for the absence of principles.

The Congress of Vienna that Talleyrand helped to organize is presented by

---

1. "La rovina di Kasch e quel che resta" by Italo Calvino, collected in *Saggi 1945–1985*. Copyright © 1995 Italo Calvino, used by permission of The Wylie Agency LLC.

Calasso as the triumph of the "constant stream of society chat, where the spies and the ladies played a role no less important than the ministers and heads of state." Need it be said that this isn't something Calasso condemns? In a world that has lost its sense of the sacred, Calasso wants to tell us, the only value that can still be realized is lightness. Talleyrand is redeemed because he presents himself as the archangel of lightness in a landscape of slaughter: albeit of a lightness that is rather programmatic, like his Mephistophelean calculations, and rather shuffling, too, like the old devil's lame leg. Better this lightness than the gravity of good intentions, which are always a harbinger of disaster: a point on which I'm in complete agreement with Calasso. The Congress of Vienna has this aspect to it, too: it's the first time "there was a concern for popular consensus," and Talleyrand here, again, is a precursor.

In describing this book, the first thing to say is that as soon as we begin reading it, we haven't gone three pages and already there are evocations of the Congress of Vienna and the salons of the Restoration superposed on the Pol Pot massacres in Cambodia. The contemporary world enters the book with the shock of a short circuit. It's no accident that Pol Pot is a subject barred from intellectual discussion, as though we were trying to forget it, because it is by no means a marginal aberration, but only the extreme apex of a mindset of ideological abstraction that has all its proliferative and clingy roots in the culture of the West: the idea that the society and the life of individuals can be manipulated like experimental material.

The Ruin of Kasch is a book that likes to present itself as a ramble, guided only by insatiable curiosity and imagination, built entirely of fragments, quotations, digressions, anecdotes, aphorisms, and so on, which are to be read with almost continual pleasure; but the premise of the book is contained in those first pages, a premise that is given, and couldn't be more serious: there's a path in front of us that is still open today, and that leads directly to the mass graves of Cambodia (an exquisitely intellectual path, in that it's based entirely on ideas, not things), and the important thing is not to avert our eyes from that point of arrival.

Does it turn out that the past was redeemed, in contrast to the modern era which is doomed? By the taking of the Bastille? No, of course not: everything was already convention and corruption long ago; the major and minor memoirists on whom Calasso draws (above all Saint-Simon) show us how spectral a world may be behind its apparently full-bodied solidity. And it's enough for Calasso to continue his exploration *à rebours* (with the Jansenists, for example) for us to see him shifting further and further upstream the poisoned sources of the "modern."

The divide is not historical but metaphysical: it's the point at which the articulation between heaven and earth (what in the sacred texts of India is called ṛta), the space in which the gods live their lives, disappears. It's difficult to establish the exact date when the abolition of this dwelling-place of the gods occurred: estimations range from the end of the Paleothic to the beginnings of the Industrial Revolution. In short, it's no longer a case of seeing History as a progression of stages in ascent or descent; instead, we might look at it as a repertory of allegories of that event, which is always present because it is always immanent.

Giving the book its title and serving as its keystone is a legend that Calasso recounts, which is adapted (how faithfully or liberally I don't know: I haven't been able to check the texts) from Leo Frobenius, the famous German ethnologist of sub-Saharan Africa. The legend concerns the ritual killing of the gods (the theme, earlier still, of Frazer's monumental work *The Golden Bough*). In the African kingdom of Naphta, the rule is that after a certain amount of time has passed, every king is killed, together with the people closest to him. The priests scan the stars every night to determine what day the sacrifice will take place. An oriental storyteller arrives at the court. His stories are so fascinating that the priests neglect their fatal observations of the firmament; the death of the king and his retinue, including the storyteller, is postponed—until ritual sacrifice falls into desuetude. The king lives to a ripe old age. The storyteller succeeds him. Then the kingdom is invaded by enemies and destroyed. The stories survive.

I said that this legend is the keystone of the book; in fact, as we keep reading, we realize that the principal theme has become the theme of sacrifice, of the function that the bloody rite has had in human civilizations, and of the ways in which the cruelty of the immolation of victims is transcended in the cultures that still understand its sacral character, or is illusorily abolished by cultures that ignore this character.

So there is sacrifice. But what about the story? The theme is less explicit, but if we look at the flood of narratives that Calasso channels through his pages, taken from chronicles and memoirs, especially French ones, from the lives and works of writers, beginning with Chateaubriand and Stendhal, and also narratives invented by him (the sources are always diligently cited in the bibliographical notes, except for a few cases where the source is evidently Calasso himself), we must conclude that, as in the desecrated kingdom of Naphta, in a Europe that no longer believes in the throne or the altar, a new production of wealth has certainly been set in motion, and that is the proliferation of stories. Does this mean that cyclical time, marked by sacrificial rites, has been succeeded by a directed, plural, and segmented time, with countless beginnings and countless independent ends—the time of the profane narrative universe that surrounds us like a forest, from the silence of the libraries to the roar of the mass media?

While it doesn't develop these ideas suggested by the legend of the storyteller and the priests, *The Ruin of Kasch* is, also, a book about literature, and everything it says on this score hits the mark. The literary equivalent of Talleyrand is Sainte-Beuve, who transforms literature into one big salon. By attaching the work to the author's person in an almost biological continuity, Sainte-Beuve stands opposed to pure literature, which emerges with Baudelaire and Flaubert. It is with these two figures that the "modern" begins to dominate even in literature, and for this Calasso ought to condemn them; but they are also the originators of that mental point of view that makes the enumeration of human *bêtise* possible; and Calasso, recognizing himself in this line that descends from them to Bloy and Kraus, offers them redemption.

There's a lot in literature that can be redeemed which in life is irredeemable. The present—uninhabitable in its very real horror—can be accepted as the pretext of a story or novel. It's no accident that Calasso dedicates several pages to that essential dimension of contemporary history: the secret services. A world of squalor and boredom in the daily headlines acquires meaning only through the mechanisms of a thriller.

The questions surrounding the sacrificial rite remain more difficult to answer than those surrounding literature. If there has apparently never been any culture in any society able to do without sacrifice, at least in the period of its formation (like all actions that seem uneconomical and answer instead to a higher idea of economy—to a contract with all the forces of the universe), this observation raises endless questions. Is it the killing of one's own kind that counts, and only as a substitute for the killing of an animal? Or is it a share of the wealth of pastoralism which requires sacrifice, like, in other cases, a share of the agricultural harvest? Is it one's own death that is being celebrated, through the identification of a sacrificer and a victim? Or is it an expiation for the carnivorous diet, through the ritualization of slaughter? And, above all, is human history dominated by doom for having neglected sacrifice and lost the notion of it, or by the attempt to transcend the practice of sacrifice, as is the case with all the major religions?

Calasso does not pronounce on these questions. But his most beautiful pages are those on the "forest doctrine" whereby the Brahmin exceeds himself by becoming "the renouncer" and refusing to eat animal flesh, thus internalizing the liturgy of the Vedas as moral law, since the sacrificial space is identified with nature itself, the destroyer and devourer, with the forest, which is alive, sacrificing the living; or the pages on the Buryats' white horse, the subject of a sacrificial rite that doesn't consist in killing the animal, but in taking off its bridle, sending it out alive into freedom, to gallop on the steppe and no longer serve man. All this with colorful rituals and ornaments and fumigations that retain the memory of its sacred significance, and its place in the continuity between heaven and earth, between the myth of the gods and the destiny of humanity, between the limitless universe and the limited human being. A continuity that doesn't indicate an absence of distinction, but a complexity of passages and articulations between worlds that refer to one another but cannot be confused.

Perhaps because this continuity is what's closest to his heart, Calasso sees his bête noire in Lévi-Strauss, the ethnologist of discontinuity, who dissects myth, separating the fluidity and density of its vital juices into dry and aseptic elements. Among the many portraits of great intellectual personalities, which are among the greatest attractions of the book (Stirner, Ricardo, Marx, Freud, et al.) and which together form a partial view of two centuries of Western cultural history, the profile of Lévi-Strauss is the one drawn with the most precise and cutting strokes. A profile faithful to the truth, yet, at the same time, I think, unjust. How much intellectual honesty there is in Lévi-Strauss—and how great his capacity for not remaining a prisoner of method—is confirmed by his latest book, *Le regard éloigné*. But what I mean to say goes beyond this. What I mean to say is that the culture of discontinuity, if nourished by an increasingly demanding analytical sensitivity, may be the only method that restores reason to the unit of humanity in the unit of the universe, and attempts to solder microcosm and macrocosm together again.

The two types of computers ("digital" and "analog"), which are currently preparing our future, represent (it's Calasso again who says it, commenting on the founder of "game theory," von Neumann) "the two poles that secretly sustain us." I agree; and I don't think there's anything left for us to do but to pursue analogical knowledge with increasingly sophisticated logical-numerical models, and to [let] the knowledge of quantities measurable by the analogic and transfigurative imagination flourish, even as we recognize that a knowledge with two poles will remain a divided knowledge, and that there will always be a residue of one unattainable for the other, and vice versa.

Translated from the Italian by Alex Andriesse

LUIS ALBERTO AYALA BLANCO

THE RUIN OF KASCH

> *It's always a suicide*
> *when something authentic dies.*
> —Nicolás Gómez Dávila

The thought of Roberto Calasso represents the last glimpse of the power left behind by the gods, when they withdrew; it outlines the silhouette of the divine order now forgotten, although present in every one of our acts. The mania for objects and verifiable data has blinkered our minds.

The power of Calasso's pen is something far from the transparency and caricaturesque autonomy of the modern; it's rather a force that emanates from a cryptic knowledge. He speaks by means of myth, metamorphic images whose reading can pass from simple delight in the language to the meaning intimated by its multiple variants. Myth only becomes palatable through an initiatory process; otherwise, it ends up devouring the sanity of those who contemplate it.

Just as Calasso says that Plato's *Republic* is an initiatory text in which "the many who did not understand, and were not supposed to understand, imagined they were reading a treatise on the perfect State,"[1] it can be said that his books, too, must be read from certain initiatory angles, or else the many who do not understand it, and are not supposed to understand it, will think that they are reading only an unparalleled display of erudition. There are times when it's not enough to be exceptionally well read to glimpse the secret

---

1. *The Marriage of Cadmus and Harmony*, 260. [All citations of Calasso's work refer, when available, to the English editions, and, when these are not available, to the original Italian editions. The bibliographical details of these editions can be found in the Reading List contained in this issue.—*Editor's Note*]

hidden in his thought; in a way it's necessary to be an initiate in order to laugh along with him, just as he does with the gods. Calasso's strength lies in his capacity for divine evocation. He converses with Athena just as Odysseus did. Nor should we forget that power derives from "possession," and that every act performed by men takes part in a divine game.

Calasso explains how the divine decides to sacrifice itself to become two, and thus initiates existence. The reason for this suicide was perhaps boredom— there must be nothing more unbearable than divine boredom—but who knows? The important thing is to understand that all creation is founded on a murder. From that moment on, the world lives an existence that, while remaining tied to the divine, enjoys a certain independence. Sacrifice is the communicating vessel between the two worlds. Man forgot it—or wanted to forget it—and with that forgetting he lost the relative freedom he had. He lives in a state of indifference with respect to the divine. But indifference doesn't guarantee the death of sacrifice. Man continues implementing it without knowing it. Nowadays, its presence is perceptible in "production." Society produces itself, i.e. sacrifices itself, through an excessive expenditure of energy—as Bataille points out—although it is now an onanistic sacrifice, addressed to itself.

Roberto Calasso's thought can hardly be labeled. It does not answer to any of the current schools or currents of thought. He is a peculiar writer. We have thinkers who've read everything but don't know what to do with it, at best using it all as a soporific. On the other hand, there are those who are noteworthy for their intelligence. Calasso is both inordinately well read and in possession of a devastating intelligence. He is a monster.

In the obsession to catalog him, there have been attempts to link him to postmodern thought. Once someone asked him whether he considered *The Marriage of Cadmus and Harmony* a postmodern book (at an event in New York with Susan Sontag and Joseph Brodsky). He replied simply: "I've never in my life felt the need to use the word Postmodern."[2] In any case, he

---

2. "World from Olympus," *The New Yorker*, April 12, 1993.

is committed to "strong" thought, in contrast to the "weak thought" championed by Gianni Vattimo.

Calasso's training is a far cry from the modern mania for specialization. Rather, in the classical manner, he is in possession of a multifold knowledge. He is perfectly at home in Greece, Vedic India, Buddhism, the nineteenth-century French, Plotinus, Nietzsche, Marx, Stirner, Heidegger, Adorno, Kraus, Freud, Benjamin, Walser, Canetti, Kafka, Baudelaire . . . to name just a few subjects.

Calasso is an initiate who plays with knowledge, not trying to propose any system, leaving that to science. Nor can we say that his books have a particular form. The most we might venture, without distorting his thinking, would be to say that he uses a mythic-analog method. But in reality, as he once said of *The Ruin of Kasch*: "I've always thought of the form as essential. So it's not a question of assembling fragments, or pages on more or less interconnected themes, but of inventing a form, which has to be born and vanish with the book."[3]

"Roberto Calasso was born in Florence in 1941 and today lives in Milan. He earned a degree in English literature at the University of Rome with Professor Mario Praz, completing a thesis entitled *The Hieroglyphics of Sir Thomas Browne*. He is editorial director and chief executive officer of the publishing house Adelphi, where he has worked since its founding in 1962."[4]

Calasso comes from a family of leftist intellectuals from the Italian haute bourgeoisie. His maternal grandfather—a friend of Benedetto Croce's—was a professor of philosophy at the University of Florence and founded the Scuola Città and the publishing house La Nuova Italia. His father was director of the Faculty of Law at the University of Rome. His mother, for her part, studied Greek literature at the University of Florence. He grew up among books. His

---

3. Alain Jaubert, "Entretien avec Roberto Calasso," *L'Infini* (Autumn 1987), 9. [Translated by Alex Andriesse.]
4. Taken from an original printing of his curriculum vitae. *The Hieroglyphics of Sir Thomas Browne* was published as a book in Mexico, in 2008, in a co-edition produced by the FCE and Sexto Piso.

childhood revolves around three libraries: that of his grandparents, that of his parents, and the Gabinetto Vieusseux, a private library in the Strozzi Palace. Thus, from childhood, the "Calasso myth" was already in motion. By thirteen, he had read all of Proust in French, and by fourteen all of Goethe in German. Regarding the young Calasso, several extraordinary anecdotes are worth noting. The most famous tells how, at the age of twenty, at Croce's daughter's house, he met one of his favorite writers: Theodor Adorno. After talking with him for a while, Adorno whispered to his hostess: "A very nice boy, he's read all my books. Including the ones I haven't yet written."[5]

Calasso was already a renowned editor before being recognized as a writer. Since the age of twenty-one, he had worked for Adelphi—founded by Luciano Foà, Roberto Bazlen, and himself—in response to the narrowness of Einaudi. Today Adelphi is one of the most important independent publishers in Europe.

Calasso combines schizophrenically—as he himself says—his life as an editor and his life as a writer. Of the latter, by the way, he does not like to say much. Maybe because of the resentment and distrust it provokes. Nobody can make sense of how, while being an editor, he finds time to write. To which he replies that he writes whenever he has a spare moment, and goes about it in a very peculiar way, first with his pen, and then transcribing it on the Olivetti typewriter that Bazlen gave him.

He is consistently attacked by the Italian left, whose members accuse him of being a right-winger. These sort of events provoke in him an irrepressible hilarity.[6] The same thing happens in academic circles: his books do not meet the requirements of good scholarly habits. But these new pietists, who

---

5. Massimo Dini, "L'insostenibile leggereza di essere Calasso," *Europeo 46*, November 13, 1992, 47.
6. "My family was one of the established families of the Italian left, he says. At five or six years old, I heard my parents discuss ideas that many people discover at twenty. When you know a thing from inside out, when you can see clearly what functions and what doesn't function in a political stance, it loses its power of enchanting." (See Andrea Lee's "Roberto Calasso's Encyclopedic Mind at Play.")

dismantle the great thinkers with their bland theses—the only thing they achieve is to provide material for fun.

The Ruin of Kasch narrates the story of the transition from one state of things to another, from the knot of necessity to the lightness of the tale-telling. It is the story of an immemorial kingdom whose order is based on sacrifice: its power is regenerated from time to time when its own death is written in the heavens. This writing prescribes the times for sacrifice and must be observed inexorably. One day, however, this order is revoked by a greater power, the power that belongs only to the lightness of chance. Then sacrifice is replaced by the nucleus, the lifeblood of the secret that it kept hidden from view: *the excess, the surplus, the total lack of support.*

In short, the order of sacrifice is brought to ruin by the essence of sacrifice. This strange turn of events leads to the unveiling of the esoteric and, with it, the end of the entire order. It's on to a world intoxicated by its own voice, woven with stories that, instead of creating an order, untie the knot that holds the forces of the cosmos together. The time is ripe for the entry of the *unlimited*, of the immoderation now present in every act of existence.

At last we are able to glimpse Calasso's secret: to know that surplus is the heart of sacrifice. The Olympians knew it, so they decided to abandon the order of Ananke and settle in the space of the simulacrum. They elected to become slight. However, with all the ambiguity that it implies, they never ceased to symbolize the limit, which is to say: *the limit is the edge of the principle of the unlimited*, the secret of the secret, that which cannot be made clear, because then the world would go crazy. And that is precisely what happens with the eruption of the power of Far-li-mas, the poet, the double, the inverted image of the stern priests in charge of observing and protecting the order prescribed in the sky: "Far-li-mas marks the beginning of another reign: the reign of the word, after that of bloodshed. It is a reign that does not kill by way of ritual, but stirs death through a rapid, indomitable disorder that supervenes. The words of Far-li-mas replace the sacrifice: like the sacrifice, they have the power to command obedience: but they don't have the power to establish time cycles. Time is now just the swing of the pendulum between one empty flow, devoid of attachments, and the suspension caused by the drug of the world. Far-li-mas's words have a power of their own, but they cannot reflect the position of the stars."[7] Undoubtedly, in the clash between the power of sacrifice and the power of story, the latter wins. Sacrifice cannot face its own foundations. In other words: sacrifice must immolate itself in order for sacrifice to continue—that is its eternal irony. Then, life is conquered by the power of the word, which can speak of everything, including secrets. But this continues to be a variant—an extreme variant—of sacrifice. However, this swan song of sacrifice has been forgotten, leading us to believe that the secular carries the day, when in reality we find ourselves at the very origin of sacrifice, now exposed, without any veil to hide it. The esoteric is experienced as banal, and this provokes the madness suffered by all forgetful men who can't explain what is happening—the way Astrabacos and Alopecos went crazy when they came across the simulacrum of the Taurian Artemis. Although this isn't even the way it is; that would be too much to hope for; it requires a certain capacity for amazement that the modern world doesn't possess. Rather, it's as though these two Spartans were carrying around the simulacrum, with all its power, the same way they might carry any old thing around. Ruin never appears as a great catastrophe, but rather as the indifferentiation of—and indifference to—the state of things.

The Ruin of Kasch narrates the transition to the complacent stupidity of the modern delineated against the blinding background of the sacred. The secret manages to prevail by means of its own disclosure, protected by modern myopia. In this way, sacrifice is carried out everywhere without anyone noticing. It is the ruin of the order, old or new—it doesn't matter. In the end, sacrifice is the pendulum swinging death between the two parties that comprise it. The victor in the ordeal is always death, disguised as life, in the game of metamorphosis.

---

7. *The Ruin of Kasch*, 144.

Talleyrand

The "great politician," Charles Maurice de Talleyrand, confines himself to giving little pushes to the wheel of events. It is not about the "will" embodied in the "historical subject," Napoleon, who restructures the cosmos from scratch. On the contrary, Talleyrand is a "master of ceremonies," capable of tuning in to events. He was a man who simply "*offered his arm* [. . .] and helped him find a way out of the embarrassment."[8] Talleyrand "from the very beginning [. . .] had recognized the mechanism of the unprecedented historical moment as something that was acting by itself. He concealed himself within it, content to tighten or loosen a screw here or there. Small 'finishing touches' in which he recognized the last kind of action that was still possible."[9] This enigmatic personage is the embodiment of the infallible politician, because he never pretended to be the man of great principles that megalomaniac modernity demanded. No one could forgive him his capacity for metamorphosis, a characteristic suspicious in the spiteful eyes of the revolutionaries, whose narrow-mindedness made them see his actions as treasonous. How else to explain that the same man was the principal player—often hidden, like the secret itself—in French policy, from the start of the Revolution through the Restoration? But he knew there was nothing to betray. Politics is simply the art of knowing how "to sniff out the times" and act according to them, a cycle of analogies and correspondences invisible to the majority. In short, all his political intelligence amounted to was "an abnormal gift for discerning how times were moving."[10] His true commitment lay in not abandoning his position as master of ceremonies. The only thing that mattered was keeping up the sacrificial order.

Talleyrand's politics are pure simulacrum, a tempestuous stream of signs:

---

8. *The Ruin of Kasch*, 14.
9. *The Ruin of Kasch*, 51.
10. *The Ruin of Kasch*, 12.

without committing to anything, he implies everything. He represents mobility, the certainty that "things no longer have a preestablished weight."[11] The secret is to be light, and to keep pace with events. Talleyrand is conscious of precariousness. The goal is to concentrate on giving little "finishing touches." Politics is the art of the ephemeral, and out of the ephemeral the warp of reality is woven. Talleyrand is not a creator of systems; he is the only one who knows how this system-proof machine works.

Now, make no mistake: Talleyrand is the great unbeliever, but he is also the creator of the beliefs necessary to maintain the bland calm of the citizenry, and so he ends up confessing that "despite being a philosopher, I deplore the progressive lack of faith in the people."[12]

Politics as the "art of the possible" means precisely this: that the politician must be responsible for pursuing the possible, without imposing their regrettable aspirations, and so seeking to establish an absolute order based on principles emanating from goddess Reason. In any case, all that's left is to play with one's surroundings and, with any luck, remain a moment longer in the torrent. What sustained Talleyrand in this mad race of events that inaugurates modernity was his awareness of the limit. The new world, into which the limitless elbows along with everything else, discovers in Talleyrand the shadow of the limit, for which, from that moment on, it will never cease to yearn.

Legitimacy is found at the origin, but can only be established after a very long time. What legitimizes legitimacy? Duration. However, what is it that legitimizes duration? Legitimacy. How to solve this problem? By being the victor in the ordeal: if a government conquers the adversities that face it, that means it has always been legitimate. On the contrary, the moment it loses, it demonstrates its illegitimacy. Victory symbolizes divine favor, and with it the ineludible facticity of any affirmation of power.

Calasso gives an example of this by quoting the words of Benjamin

---

11. *The Ruin of Kasch*, 33.
12. Talleyrand, quote in *The Ruin of Kasch*, 92.

Constant in *De l'esprit de conquête et de l'usurpation*, differentiating despots from usurpers. The latter abandon power legitimized by the divine challenge. They represent the group of politicians at the Congress of Vienna, whose "most perverse achievement has been to wipe out the expanse of time over which monarchs had given *douceur* to their power."[13] This *douceur* was the bond of the sacred correspondences: the investiture.

The despot wields power ruthlessly, but that is his objective and he does not attempt to justify it. Investiture itself gives him the necessary legitimacy. The usurper, like the despot, wields power arbitrarily—there is really no other way to wield it, anything else is cowardice—but unlike the despot, he needs to be shrouded by the approbation of others. He cannot face the crudeness of power, and in his need to justify it makes it much harder to bear. Not only does he end up debasing what the people revered, but by destroying the hierarchical order, by cutting ties with the sacred, power has to augment its strength, becoming increasingly cruel. After all, the power of the usurper aggravates the despotic structure by pretending that everything is done by consensus.[14]

The Congress of Vienna can be summed up as the image of a group of usurpers presided over by Talleyrand, acting as master of ceremonies. It inaugurates politics as the distribution of spoils. Talleyrand knew this game of pillage must be concealed behind the cloak of great principles; that the outbreak of excess should be conducted, even if only in a simulated way, along the ceremonial path that refers to origins. It didn't matter that no one had faith in him; he still had to go on presenting himself as a starting point for any political action. It was the only way to keep playing, without the game collapsing due to stubborn modern arrogance. Talleyrand's task as the "master of ceremonies" of all modern politics boils down to the following: keep up the style, i.e. without ever ceasing to metamorphose, so that belief doesn't leave us, just as, in their time, the gods used to do.

---

13. *The Ruin of Kasch*, 41–42.
14. *The Ruin of Kasch*, 41–43.

The Forgetting of Sacrifice

The modern world is a huge slaughterhouse . . . and doesn't know why. The springs of sacrifice continue setting the wheel of events in motion, but now they do so concealed behind the veil of indifference. Impossible to understand today's world except from this perspective.

Calasso, with his usual irony, shows how we live among the remnants of the forgetting of sacrifice, and how sacrifice continues to perpetuate itself in the cracks of our blindness. His criticism is devastating because he is not resentful, he doesn't pretend to prescribe how things should be, and, most importantly, at no time does he disparage the target of his criticism; he concentrates simply on playing with the light—enlightened? illuminated?—emitted by the ambient inanity; it is an affirmative game that has no need to involve itself with the inevitable bitterness of any talk of the "truth."

The forgetting of sacrifice exacerbates itself, so that sacrifice returns in secular forms, such as experimentation and production. "Experimentation is a sacrifice in which guilt has been expunged. The sacrificial pyramid, where blood has drenched the warm stones of the altar, becomes a vast slaughterhouse that extends horizontally in some nondescript corner of the city. [. . .] The peculiarly modern form of sacrifice is a vast industrial undertaking that shuns the name and memory of sacrifice. There is talk of whole classes to be eliminated, or otherwise of those inevitable dropouts who each day are cast out of the social mechanism. But they are always events strictly belonging to society." The power of sacrifice is greatest precisely when one tries to eradicate it. It is an ellipse in whose trajectory the way of correspondences is erased and supplanted by the sandy clearing of equality. If, earlier, sacrifice relied on a "way of action," which protected it from indifferentiation, now sacrifice is performed everywhere and at every moment. It no longer relies on difference; it is no longer the correspondence of the precise act at the precise moment; it is the equivalence that allows the standardization of everything, juxtaposing what is different as though it were the same, regardless of the moment. There is no possibility of distinguishing those who know from those who do not know. Now everyone acts as if they knew without knowing. We live in a state of "forced esotericism." "The way of action," which corresponded with gnosis—"the way of being conscious of actions"—has worn away, and the consciousness that only some possessed is stripped bare, everyone participates in it, everyone knows inadvertently, although they do not know it. They live out the end of the secret: *believing everything is permitted without going through an initiation process.* Which is to say, now everybody claims that they know, and that they have the right to know, what the initiates guarded as their most precious treasure. Let us not forget that one of the vices of democracy, as Cioran rightly said, is to allow any old imbecile to govern.

If, earlier, sacrifice was supposed to "repeat the irreversible,"[15] now it only stammers equivalencies. But that's exactly why it's everywhere. The moment there is no god to sacrifice, and no object worthy of being sacrificed . . . the moment the other part is forgotten, sacrifice leaks into every act, completely inundating what was intended to negate it. "The first consequence of forgetting sacrifice is that the world will then be used without restraint, without limit, without any part being dedicated to any other. But here, too, the end is superimposed upon the beginning, like a reflection, and therefore seen in reverse. Once the sacrifice has disappeared, the whole world, without realizing it, goes back to being an immense sacrificial laboratory."[16]

Forgetting the divine . . . forgetting the sacrifice, which for the moment has been swapped for simple obfuscation. It is not even the forgetting; it's the certainty in the truth which exposes the contemporary world as an immense sacrificial laboratory. As if the gods could be required to be true! As if there were "one" truth! As if the truth could be a substitute for the divine! Nietzsche has already had enough to say about how naive it is to cling to the truth, the last bastion of the fainthearted. And they credulously

---

15. *The Ruin of Kasch*, 208.
16. *The Ruin of Kasch*, 149–50.

cling to the truth of their autonomy: the autonomy of a fragment that divinity itself lopped off, in order to be two and not one. Hence the guilty origin of existence: "The purpose of sacrifice is not to atone for guilt, as we read in the textbooks. Sacrifice *is* guilt, the only guilt."[17] Guilt is at the root and it's an irrevocable decision; let's not forget that it was made by the victim, who thus became his own executioner. The divine cannot and does not want to expiate itself, whatever secular cant may claim. Guilt is to want to be two: it means the birth of life conceived through suicide. It is the death of the one transfigured into the multiple. It is the birth of the exchange, the metamorphosis of the same into an endless game of masks. Before the creation, before the primordial murder, before the divine suicide, otherness did not exist; indeed, there was no existence. The divine was not even aware of itself. Through sacrifice, divinity comes into contact with itself by way of the part it left floating in the void. From that moment on, sacrifice is performed unrelentingly.

The whole game of existence oscillates between a give and a take. Man offers the divinity a part of the world, so that it will "give him the rest of the world, and no longer [. . .] intervene there with its uncontrollable whim."[18] However, it never entirely happens. At any moment, the divine might regain control. The important thing is to know that the exchange must continue, that sacrifice is the shackle that imprisons man, without ceasing to be the only possibility of enjoying a certain kind of freedom. That is why it is a duality characterized by the correspondence between victim and executioner, and by the reversibility of both in the theater of existence: a specular process wherein divinity is recognized by its shadow.

Sacrifice is the death of oneself in order to become another; it alludes to exchange, and thereby to substitution. "It is said that sacrifice is the origin of exchange: but exchange is the set in which sacrifice is a subset: and exchange, in turn, is included in another category—substitution—which alone makes

---

17. *The Ruin of Kasch*, 145.
18. *The Ruin of Kasch*, 149.

it possible: this *stands for* that: the one who *gives* this *takes* that."[19] The executioner returns and the victim remains lying there, lifeless. The death of the other symbolizes my own death. The correspondences that comprise the whole body of the divine thus establish it.

The emphasis is on the death of the victim and the violence done to the victim. The important thing is the gift, offering the irreversible: the secret of the secret of sacrifice. The offering is that part which never returns—time— the surplus that the divine sought after becoming two. Irreversibility, difference, the decision to cease being one . . . there you have the secret that has been lost in this warehouse of copies called modernity.

The gods appropriate the prototype, the irreducible, unique part. But we must be careful not to confuse it with the Platonic mold. No, the unique is irreversible precisely because it does not participate in any archetype: it is an image lost in its own appearance. The "unique" is the eternity of the instant, the eternity of the ephemeral, and not the ephemeral of any claim to duration. Sacrifice seeks to "repeat the irreversible," the surplus, "the accursed share" that everyone wants, including the gods. However, it is now concealed under certain secular names. "The foundation of the inversion: society is able to absorb within it all divine as well as natural images: all that which stood *in front of* society, from which society was detached, with which it negotiated at every moment of its life."[20]

Society appropriates the structure of the divine, negating it. Absorbs its essence in order to spit it out, aseptically, transparently, without any secrets, in a single direction—progress. Thanks to this, Durkheim can say: "the religious is the social." A mutation of the divine into its caricatured double, with society as the only referent: "The unnamable present."[21] But the gods aren't dumb. This is the latest prank they're playing on us. They're relying on scientific stupidity

---

19. *The Ruin of Kasch*, 152.
20. *The Ruin of Kasch*, 155.
21. *The Ruin of Kasch*, 267. *The Unnamable Present* is Calasso's most recent book, published by Adelphi in 2017.

to let them keep on laughing in anonymity. The true cunning of the gods consists in having made Prometheus believe they'd been fooled, when all they did was force men to contend, in order to go on living, with death and hunger, while they were busy breathing in the fumes of sacrifice. The gods know that in the excess, the fortuitousness, the pointlessness that luxury entails, the pleasure of existence is found, and that the rest—the fodder of science, the verifiable—is only food for worms. Calasso reminds us that "the gods hidden in the unknown know that the most valuable gifts do not belong to that category: happiness, above all, is unverifiable, uncontrollable, and unrepeatable."[22] Durkheim's axiom is victim to a terrible irony: when the secular seemed to take possession of the divine, a sound of quiet laughter hints that everything has been just one more game played by the gods, who even in their retirement continue having fun at our expense. They recreate themselves in their eternal game. We strive to break free from the Promethean deception, exorcise the irreversible: to kill and eat . . . The irreversible, the esoteric itself, the secret of the secret, we experience as just one more banality. Because we're so close we can't see it. It is hidden by transparency, by impenetrable, pornographic theology. And this has its price: even as the gods play, we wear ourselves thin in the search for the lost meaning of the obvious.

The gods offered us life in exchange for distracting them from divine boredom. It is impossible to forget that transgression is always transgression of radical alterity . . . of the sacred. Whether we act like buffoons or accursed children, we will be marked by the fatality of this ineludible bond—sacrifice—which links us to the divine.

---

22. *The Ruin of Kasch*, 157.

The Post-Historical Individual

The post-historical individual is the *lumpen* hated and despised by Marx, that hybrid of ultimate promise and absolute disenchantment. But what is Calasso referring to when he says "post-history"? To the inversion of the world, the absorption of everything into a single entity: society. Again, everything is related to everything, but now it's an autistic, decontextualized, or, rather, hysterical relationship, which out of fear of being seduced seeks to be the sole seducer. "History: transformations (events described in history books) happen *against* an order that presents itself as stable. It is an order of substances, of correspondences, of analogies. The invisible, omnipresent, inevitable axis of the world. Post-history: transformations are implicit in the experimental nature of order, which presents such character as stable."[23] And its inhabitants are those individuals described by Max Stirner in *The Ego and Its Own*. They personify the incarnation of disenchantment, but not the gentle disenchantment professed by the romantics; the disenchantment that wallows in its own feces, and no one else's, which is to say: a disenchantment devoid of nostalgia. They do not depend on anything, they are unique, and free from memory . . . except for resentment, as Nietzsche showed.

However, that is still a version of man that might have something salvageable about it. At least these people live out their denial cynically, unceremoniously, without the annoying pretense of justifying their actions and their stupidity—and that is something. As opposed to that other group of individuals who spring from the same source: proud of their autonomy, but without the get-up-and-go to finish expelling the sacred, they transmute it into new beliefs. As Calasso points out, Stirner is forgiven everything, except for having exposed the secular world's sanctimoniousness, the failed attempt to do away with the sacred, or, worst of all, for showing how the secular presents

---

23. *The Ruin of Kasch*, 157.

itself as a distorted tic of the sacred. Here, Stirner is withering: "Our atheists are pious people."[24]

At least in the sphere of the divine, there was room for heresy. There was something to transgress. Evil had a point of reference, which gave it value. With any luck, even the gods themselves would take charge of doing away with us. Which is to say, you had the option to stop believing. The pious people Stirner alludes to don't even doubt; they retain a blind faith in their unbelief. Calasso lashes out with devastating lucidity: "What is more sanctimonious, indeed, than a healthy layman, so conceited and credulous in his principles? [. . .] And Enlightened thinkers? If they really do exist, they should first of all stop believing in the Enlightenment. These are the new 'pious people,' whose sanctimony is not even protected by the mediation of ceremony, by the arcane pragmatism of a church. Rather than being governed by a sacrament, they let themselves be possessed by capital letters: Society, Humanity, Mankind, the Species—these were the nineteenth-century favorites that still plague the present day, though many others have been added."[25]

The "unique" person is also Dostoyevsky's underground man, or the homunculus with which Cioran had so much fun in his aphorisms. He is a worm, wriggling through the passageways of his own impotence, wreaking havoc every time he sees a difference, a threat. This man is everywhere, in universities, in companies, and from time to time he goes out to soak up some sun in the street; he lives engrossed in his stupidity, worshipping everything that allows him to keep on wriggling. The most serious cases are found in sanctuaries of knowledge. These are not only pious people; they are the new priests, the Enlightened thinkers described by Calasso. And in their caricature of impartiality, shrouded by hieratical gestures, they guard their ignorance of everything they do not understand, everything that is not scientific. Their disbelief is so great that, even when someone confronts them with some vestige of wisdom, they deny it, because it never manages to pass their pathetic verification test.

---

24. Quoted in *The Ruin of Kasch*, 285.
25. *The Ruin of Kasch*, 285.

That is the sanctimoniousness reigning nowadays in the world. They really are unique! If only they had the strength to smite the cosmos, to assert themselves in defiance of the gods, to explode the sacrificial order into a thousand pieces and live as nomads among the fragments that remain in the air, without then pretending to adopt the structure of the sacred—all the while denying it—it would be a different story. At least they'd be able to boast of a majestic moment, and thus gain the respect of the gods.

Translated from the Spanish by Gabriel Abramowicz

JOSEPH BRODSKY

THE MARRIAGE OF CADMUS AND HARMONY[1]

The first thing I'd like to say about this book is that it should be immediately issued in paperback.

The second is that the pleasure of seeing this book is next only to the pleasure of writing it; and I, for one, am practically mad at its author for depriving me of this pleasure.

The third is that this book is impossible to review, for either praise or criticism of it will be criticism or praise from below.

This is the kind of book one comes across only once or twice in one's lifetime. I'd say—once, as I am not that young.

One may liken this book to Apollonius of Rhode's *Argonautica*, to Ovid's *Metamorphosis* [sic], or to Robert Graves's *The White Goddess*, but that would be missing the point by an awfully wide margin.

We deal here not with human but with divine repetition, which—repetition, that is—for God is a sign of majesty, as Calasso says; and, I'd add, of viability.

Calasso's book is neither a compendium of mythology, nor an attempt to construct a personal universe.

It's neither factual nor fanciful. It's not an attempt to domesticate the incomprehensible for the purposes of popular consumption, and it's not an essayistic fantasy in the continental mode on the subject of cultural nostalgia. It's not a *texte*, for all its *plaisirs*.

It's not the product of a particularly esoteric philosophy, nor is it a stylish escape from the mental vulgarity of the present by means of intellectual coquetry.

---

1. Copyright © 1993 Joseph Brodsky and used by permission of The Wylie Agency LLC.

(It's a totally free, devoid, I'd say of any jargon—Freudian, structuralist, deconstructionist, you name it—although this is the lousiest compliment to pay this book.)

The Marriage of Cadmus and Harmony is a book about the etymology and morphology of existence, because that's what mythology essentially is.

A commentary on mythology. This book is therefore a commentary on two governing principles of human existence—of necessity and chance—on their interplay and their provenance.

To regard Greek antiquity as humankind's childhood is about as idiotic as to regard the present as humankind's maturity. Greek mythology is not a naive, animistic, pantheistic version of the universe but the sanest available vision of the existential fabric, with its holes, stains, and fringes quivering in the darkness.

Mr. Calasso's book is not so much an effort to smooth its wrinkles or wash the cloth as the keen—relentless, at times—scrutiny of these holes, stains, and especially fringes, for darkness is yet another cloth.

Life, as Susan Sontag once remarked, is a movie; death is a photograph. In the context of such a metaphor, mythology, as well as theogony itself, could easily be likened to television, especially given the distinct anthropomorphic see-saw which is at work in both.

The scale and the parameters are quite different, of course; but self-projection is self-projection. Besides, the seat of either is one's home, or, more accurately, one's mind. An altar is, as it were, a box. Sacrifice could be regarded as remote control. Mount Olympus had twelve channels.

But the resemblance is limited; in fact, it stops earlier. For mythology, whether as man's self-projection upon infinity, or vice versa, is, above all, the quest for causality.

As systems of causality go, mythology is far more rewarding than anything else available, because it is supremely open-ended and because its chief structural pattern is neither a direct line nor a spiral but a zigzag.

Evidently, the Greeks had an extraordinary metaphysical appetite, an appetite for the infinite, which made them realize that the rationality of discourse doesn't guarantee the rationality of the subject.

Intuitively, I imagine, they have concluded that direct linear thinking results in a narrowing of the perspective, as well as of the existential options. Aristotle's, and Anaximander's insistence on the finality of the inquiry is but an echo of this conclusion.

By this token, tracing the emergence of our universe to the big bang, or that of our species to the monkey or amoeba, is a narrowing of perspective.

Apart from the absence of the proper instruments, the Greeks wouldn't have arrived at such conclusions, if only because such conclusions would be for them of no import.

Where we see the end of the line they saw or sought an explanation. Hence their divinities' interplay with mortals, which could be dubbed a chthonic expansion; hence, too, those divinities' proclivity for detachment, i.e., their cosmic expansion.

The odd, almost terrifying aspect of Calasso's book is that its author appears to be more keen on and sure of the cosmic than the chthonic. That is, he displays almost a greater appetite for the infinite than for the finite. It is as if his mind is more subject to the outward gravitational pull than the earthward.

He, of course, might retort that Zeus himself seldom dealt with his brother Hades—only when the latter decided to get married to Persephone. I accept that. Nevertheless, the ease and the readiness of Mr. Calasso to betake himself, at the slightest stirring, to the remotest, the most opaque reaches of detachment, is almost chilling.

But then, he follows gods; and what's chilling for us is, for gods, liberating. For as much as they like the mortals they cherish their freedom. Perhaps the main characteristic of gods is that their carnality is matched by the extremes of their detachment.

This book is, of course, about both. It is about the immortals' interplay with the mortals. More exactly, about the infinite's interplay with the finite. That's how the Greeks thought about their life, and this book warps time and puts us into their midst.

An odd thing is that one feels comfortable in those surroundings. This is largely because the nature of the human predicament and enterprise hasn't changed significantly in the interim. Yet it is also because in the author, we have a supremely informed guide—a Virgil, really, bearing in mind that he too has borrowed the conceit from Homer.

If only because this book deals with what we regard as the past, it is destined to have the future. But mythology is not the past. Mythology—like the meaning of life—escapes history, and it's a writer who flings the door of history open to follow it.

The Greeks would have recognized Roberto Calasso as one of their own. Not only because, as Italians say, *stessa faca, stessa rassa* [sic]—but in the same way as they would have recognized Ovid or Nonnus—those through whom their civilization lingered beyond the confines of its history.

Is this, then, the work of a mediterranean [sic] genius? Of a genius, that's certain. And it's all Calasso's own, unless, of course, one assumes that it is one of their gods—say, Apollo—who has entered Roberto Calasso's frame to tell their inside story—for, on occasion, you hear in these pages an extremely intimate, yet at the same time highly impersonal timbre, which cannot belong to one of us and which is not the result of translation, either.

No, it's not the translator's. Tim Parks, a superb English novelist—the best, frankly, among the modern writers of fiction—has done an absolutely splendid job. So, reluctantly, one has to put it down to the unique genius of Roberto Calasso, who, toward the end of this millennium, opened himself up to "one of their gods" and let that god's voice interfere with his own, let himself become that god's, or those gods', mouthpiece.

I use this expression—one of their gods—because this is the title of a poem by Constantine Cavafy, in which he tells you how to recognize a god in the crowd—for gods tend to mingle with mortals. Although a god may be dressed in a fairly ordinary manner, the telling sign, says Cavafy, is "the joy of knowing that he is immortal in his eyes."

To that we should add that his voice is not thunder but usually a mixture of the intimate and the impersonal; that he doesn't explain myths but rather lets myths explain life; that he tells you that infinity and finality are related in an extraordinarily complex manner: like molecules, perhaps, or words themselves.

When you meet somebody who answers these characteristics, you had better step back and let him pass, for he may be a god.

Or else you are seeing Mr. Roberto Calasso. Of course, if one of these characteristics is lacking, than you deal with just a hero—Achilles, say, or Hercules.

In any case, I suggest you take a closer look at this book's author, for he, I think, is less mortal than most of us. His book certainly is.

On page 102 it contains what may well amount to its epigraph. Describing the deportment of the Homeric hero, Calasso says:

> Before the hour strikes, he achieves a vision of things as sharply sep-
> arate from one another and complete in themselves as though scis-
> sored from the sky by cosmic shears and thrust out into a light from
> which there is no escape.

With the immanent logic of metamorphosis, this depiction turns into the author's or, if you will, his book's, self-portrait.

New York, March 1993

PIETRO CITATI

FROM MOUNT OLYMPUS, THE GODS DESCEND . . .

The modern idea of myth was born one hundred and sixty years ago, at the heart of that parodic encyclopedia of all the styles of all of universal history called *Faust II*. In the *Klassische Walpurgisnacht*, the second act of *Faust II*, the Greek myths are dead. Goethe summons their ghosts upon the stage of his illusionist theater. For one night, by the light of the moon, the ghosts return to life: once more they become the Cabeiri and the Telchines, Nereid and Proteus, the Graeae and Helen. Every one of them bears, like an archeological stamp, the precise echo of his time: they are no longer immortal: we know when they were born and when they died: and the poet's gesture fixes and parodies them. Then, with an act of supreme vivification, Goethe imbues these grotesque, temporalized ghosts with the timeless halo of the archetype. All modern mythology, all the parodies and disguises, all the pastiches and ironies à la Eliot, are descended from these marvelous lines.

For Yeats, as for Roberto Calasso, who has devoted a very beautiful book to Greek mythology (*The Marriage of Cadmus and Harmony*), myth has never died. Myth is the Unknown Guest, the Veiled Traveler, who wanders among us just as it did in the days of Homer and the *polis*. It has never ceased to be alive: it has never lost its allure for mankind; and just now it's enjoying a particular vitality, because the multifaceted psychology of modern man and his non-temporal sense of time are bringing him closer than ever to the mythical condition.

Among the stories he collects, Calasso never chooses the oldest version, the "true" version, the institutionalized version, discounting the "false" versions, as so many scholars do. Myth is, for him, a single body, a unique organism, vibrant, resonant, and ambiguous, which was never born and will never die, and where everything is connected with everything else.

He offers us infinite variations on every story, all contradicting each other. These variants are all equally correct: Homer and Hesiod have the same authority as Claudian or Nonnus or a Byzantine scholiast or a seventeenth-century savant or Gustave Moreau or a madman who, in a café in Paris or Rome, claims to be Hermes. If, following a hidden path, accompanied by the Veiled Traveler, we enter into the mythical condition, if we understand that Apollo and Dionysus and Atreus and Cadmus are the forms of our existence, then we, too, possess the authority of Homer. Like him, we can invent myths: tell them again, offer new variants, color them, set them to music, transform them, as Calasso has dared to do.

Not all of the stories recounted by writers or depicted by poets are truly myths. Some are only literary transcriptions that no longer contain the thrill of the sacred. How many times have the figures of Apollo and Artemis, or of Achilles and Helen, been offended by those who celebrate them! There is only one way to happen on an authentic myth. We are reading a book: we are following a figure to whom many contradictory and incompatible adventures are attributed: it seems that nothing can unify them: we are on the point of condemning this jumble of fragments. And then we realize that a tightly woven, superhuman music is encroaching on these apparently random events. A gift for philology or history is not enough. It takes a sixth sense to apprehend this aura, this mysterious irradiation, this assonance, this magical network between earth and heaven, which was once called Hermes, and Apollo, and Artemis, and Achilles. "That stone in the Argos, that constellation in the sky, that hanging corpse, that death by childbirth, that girl with an arrow through her breast: Ariadne was all of this."

Like every modern writer, Calasso dreams of the archaic form of the divine—when it was stone, smoke, tree, animal, and nothing of its form mixed with our own. But Calasso isn't prone to any humanist or classicist fallacies. He is very well aware that the humanization of the gods (or better: the disguising of the divine in human form) was the most dangerous of events for man, because from then on the gods began to hide themselves, to erase their completeness, to toy terribly with the creatures that resembled them. Suddenly, men felt their breath on their necks. And simultaneously, they realized that the distance between them and the gods had grown, becoming unbridgeable, in the apparent resemblance of their forms.

All that remained was to accept this distance, and to suffer. Those who wanted to erase it (like the saints and the poets) could only leap into a vortex of ecstasy and annulment, toward the *tremendum*, which constitutes the essence of the divine. They wanted to be violated, possessed, and destroyed by this immense dark light, which expressed itself through rape. But only then, in the moment of consummation and completion, did they experience the rapture, the possession, the sacred *mania*. "When something undefined and powerful shakes mind and fiber and trembles the cage of our bones, when the person who only a moment before was dull and agnostic is suddenly rocked by laughter and homicidal frenzy, or by the pangs of love, or by the hallucinations of form, or finds his face streaming with tears, then the Greek realizes that he is not alone. Somebody else stands beside him, and that somebody is a god."

I cannot trace all the themes, the analyses, and the illuminations of a book so dense, which I would suggest reading very slowly, as you would read the cyclical books or the *Metamorphoses* of Ovid. One very beautiful theme is that of the hero, who lives mythically, as every one of us should live. His ego bores him: he becomes another, many others: if he is Alexander, he becomes Achilles and Dionysus, Hercules and Cyrus the Great: his gestures repeat gestures of greater antiquity, which in turn suggest infinite gestures and echoes in the modern era; and in this dizzy blur of "I" and models and echoes, the hero enters the timeless place, or is in danger of losing himself forever. Another motif is the link between necessity and play; and another that of the woolen strips, symbols of the "connection of everything with everything," which alone gives a meaning to life; and another that of the veil, the ultimate object we encounter in Greece. "Beyond the veil, there is no other thing. The veil is the other. It tells us that the existing world, alone, cannot hold, that at the very least it needs to be continually covered and discovered, to appear and disappear."

The Marriage of Cadmus and Harmony presupposes an immense culture. Calasso has read all things Greek, or is somehow tapped in to Greece: Homer, Aeschylus, Plato, Aristophanes—and the last Byzantine scholiasts and the medieval encyclopedists and the seventeenth-century mythographers and the extravagant scholars of the nineteenth century, in whom one could still find an echo of what Cadmus, for the first time, put forth in words. In each of the book's aphorisms, the whole of Greece is present. The immense body of mythology—all the gods and demigods and heroes and metamorphoses—palpitates and shines and assaults us in every line. Calasso has an all-encompassing gaze: the gift of the eagle, who sees a very broad space from his high observatory, and the gift of the ant, who knows every blade of grass, flower, and stone in his own more minimal terrain. Without this alternation between or inhabiting the gaze of both eagle and ant, Greece—and perhaps any other subject as well—would forever elude observation.

In *The Ruin of Kasch*, his previous book, Calasso spoke of myths, though without the mythic disposition. Now, here, after an immersion and a rapture of many years, he possesses it perfectly, and he has become an active member in the golden chain that leads from Homer to who knows where and who knows when. With his vampiric, octopus-like gift, he transforms the holdings of a very long tradition into his own material: he transcribes and retells, even as he injects his own inventions into the old body. The mixture of fidelity and invention, transcription and reconstruction, seems to me perfect—so much so that, in the end, not even a connoisseur would be able to distinguish between what Calasso has interpreted and what he has invented. *The Marriage* is a book without any real modern parallels. Imagine a combination of Ovid's *Metamorphoses*, Nonnus's *Dionysiaca*, Apollodorus's *Bibliotheca*, and one of the great seventeenth-century repertories that inspired Goethe and Keats.

Everything analytic and interpretive is hidden among the folds of a narrative that seems entirely self-sufficient. Many readers will let themselves be seduced by the melody of the text, as if Calasso were only a crazed storyteller; few will notice that the interpretation, concentrated and hidden, irradiates and infects the surfaces. But one choice he makes is remarkable. The myth's proper form is the story which doesn't end and can never end, like Ulysses's story, which keeps the Phaeacians awake through the night. Calasso has disposed with the continuous storytelling of cosmogonies and rituals and instead fitted together aphorisms, tales, and anecdotes. His muse is the web, the repetition of comings and goings, the labyrinth. Yet we never get the impression that these things are "fragmentary" because, behind the fragments, there's re-emergent a sense of inexhaustible fluidity—a sense which is the very lifeblood of mythology, when it decides to appear.

What a soft, subtle, voluptuous, obdurate gaze accompanies the affairs of gods and heroes. There is never a change of pace. A slow, monotonous, melodic prose follows the stories, for the gods weren't born until writing had been invented. With increasingly sinuous and enveloping gestures, Calasso encroaches on the enigma: he untangles it; and then, just when we are about to close the book, he ties it up and knots it again, so that the Greek world goes back into hiding, in its unapproachable darkness.

Translated from the Italian by Alex Andriesse

CHARLES MALAMOUD

ON ROBERTO CALASSO'S *KA*

I want to say first of all that, with *Ka*, Roberto Calasso has given us a profound and brilliant book that has bewitched me. But I also must say there is something disconcerting, something disquieting that I have to try to define. In fact, I am wrong to say "but," for it seems to me that this disconcerting aspect of the work is part of its charm. It is not a work of scholarship, it is not an essay, and it is not a book of Indian mythology explained for Europeans. It is a vast montage that takes the form of a story, comprising a meditation on the notion of story, or rather a meditation on India *as* story.

Indeed, what the specialist remarks and the lay reader senses is that the work—mysterious as the personage who lends it its name—is much closer to scholarship than it may seem, and at the same time much more a literary creation than one may think.

More scholarly: the list of textual references that occupy pages 465 to 471 include only direct quotations. But it is worth knowing that almost half the entire book is made up of a sort of rewriting—often very close to the original version—of passages of Sanskrit texts that introduce us to the essential myths, and also of a re-elaboration of analyses done by Indologists. Roberto Calasso's narrations are based on an immense store of knowledge: the treasures of Indian mythology such as they are preserved in sometimes forbiddingly long and often obscure texts, as well as the culture of Indology. Calasso has masterfully assimilated the work of generations of Sanskritists from the nineteenth century on. And we must not lose sight of the fact that Calasso demonstrates the same mastery, the same encyclopedic knowledge of the domains of ancient Greek and European literature.

For my part—and to confine myself to my own field—I must say that I have rarely had such an attentive reader, so quick to fathom what I was striving to think through and show. To take only one example of Calasso's covert erudition, the reader should be aware that Chapter One of Ka is a reprise—in the form of a very deft and scrupulous summary—of chapters fifteen to fifty-three of the first book of the *Mahābhārata*, which together form what is called the Book of Astika, an autonomous outgrowth within the frame story that encircles and sets up the immense central narrative of the war between the Kauravas and the Pandavas. This is the case throughout the book: everything that Calasso says is based on a specific text, a text that he has had to identify, excerpt, comprehend, and recompose. And it's here that scholarly reading is combined with literary creation, is transformed into literary creation. The writer's freedom lies in the cutting and montage of stories whose sequence is not determined by thematic or historical considerations, but by a causality reminiscent of the causality of dreams. These are, besides, singular stories that themselves, owing to their structure and also to the tone Calasso has managed to adopt, often display the paradoxes of oneiric logic.

Apart from the selection and modification of the tales, and the way one slips into the next, where does the writer intervene? It is above all in his embroidering on the thoughts and feelings of mythic characters, his development of hints that the texts give about this subject while remaining in a certain sense on the outside. The writer, by quite simple but subtle procedures, creates or amplifies these characters' subjectivity, for example by having them soliloquize. Thus the writer-narrator can also allow himself a few ironically anachronistic inspirations, a few psychologizing notations, which often work wonderfully, and when they do recall Thomas Mann's approach in the fiction that he, in his turn, dedicated to India, entitled *The Transposed Heads*.

The writer's freedom is also apparent in the way he interlaces story and commentary, mediated by a comparison that recalls the process of "coalescence," *kleśāh*, specific to Sanskrit rhetoric. Thus the book's final section. Here, it's a question of a tree characteristic of Hindu culture and of a tree characteristic of Buddhist tradition. Calasso brings up the story of the confusion between these two trees in order to tell us (1) that in India, from Vedic times until the days of Buddhism, everything derives from a single trunk, and (2) that in India what can be called the Tree of Life and what can be called the Tree of Knowledge (they are not presented as such in the Indian tradition) are one and the same tree, or, seen closer up, two trees inextricably enlaced.

But what is even more notable, and more consequential—and which shows how the modern writer's narrative process illustrates essential but seldom formulated themes of Indian thought—is the way Calasso begins his text: "Suddenly an eagle darkened the sky." Only a modern can permit himself to begin like this: "Suddenly . . ." In fact this word, far from being an introduction, describes an abrupt change, which presupposes without specifying an anterior fact. This creates a context for utterance quite different from the classical beginnings: "in those days," or "once upon a time," or "in the beginning," or "in the year such and such," or " when X had reached his twentieth year," and so on—all beginnings that consist in marking a place in the continuum of time.

Here the beginning, through the rupture it introduces, reveals itself to be a first cut, an act of violence, an interruption of a preexisting situation, and therefore not, in the strictest sense, a beginning. A story from ancient India could not *begin* in this way. But the idea that something necessarily exists prior to any imaginable beginning and that to begin is simultaneously to *break in* and to *take up again* is implicit in the craftsmanship of its discursive texts. Several in fact begin with the formula, "Then, consequently" (*athatas*), and the commentaries explain that a text can only be the continuation or consequence of texts that precede it. And it's the same with cosmogonies: even those that teach us that in the beginning there was neither being nor non-being hasten to offer us a genealogy of that initial indifferentiation.

So, the sky darkens suddenly because an immense eagle, newly hatched, has just taken wing. It shows remarkable literary skill to make the beginning of this series of stories not what is most ancient—the Veda—but what is most central. The reader thereby obtains a synchronic, eagle-eyed view, from the heights of the sky. It can therefore be seen that the true hero of these stories is less the god Ka, a question personified, who outlives all the answers that might abolish him, than the Vedic hymn X, 121, which provides the poetic and ritual texture.

What are these stories? Myths, of course. But what are they supposed to teach us? In the terms of Brahmanic India at least, they are not parables or edifying tales. If there are lessons to be drawn from them, they are not truths about the meaning of life, the mysteries of death, virtues and vices, but about the knowledge of notions so fundamental it is as though they were buried at the heart of utterance—notions of the distance between the same and the different, and thus about continuity and non-repetition: in Sanskrit, *samtati* and *ajamitva*. There are myths that are like elementary illustrations of ritual facts. So it is with the story of Aditi giving birth to Asura, a story that Calasso does not fail to narrate, on page 243. So, too, with the myth that has made such a deep impression on me that for the past two decades I have several times made it the subject of my publications: the myth that describes how the god Indra prevents congress between the Rite and the Word, violates the Word in order to be reborn of the Word and to ensure the exclusivity of this rebirth[1]— thereby proving that the gods are only what is said of them, and in the final analysis are only the question, Ka?, which arises with regard to the one who is their origin.

Translated from the French by Alex Andriesse

---

1. Indra, in order to prevent the birth of a monster produced by the union between the Word (*vāc*) and the Rite (*yajna*), enters the Word's womb. [Editor's Note]

WENDY DONIGER

INDIA AND EUROPE IN *KA: STORIES OF THE MIND AND GODS OF INDIA*

When Roberto Calasso was writing *Ka: Stories of the Mind and Gods of India*, that he published in 1998, he had already written *The Ruin of Kasch* (1994), which interpreted a sacrifice in ancient India in the light (or, more precisely, the darkness) of the French revolution. In *Ka*, Calasso remained ostensibly within the bounds of India, but he tied together all the fragments of Hindu mythology into a continuous, readable, intensely detailed story, in which the shadow of Europe in the form of Calasso's own imagination, the imagination of a highly original, literate, creative Italian publisher, still fell upon the text in more subtle ways. We can see that invisible presence in the very opening of the book:

> Suddenly **an eagle** darkened **the sky.** Its bright black, almost violet feathers made a moving curtain between clouds and earth. Hanging from its claws, likewise immense and stiff with terror, **an elephant and a turtle skimmed the mountain**tops. It seemed the bird meant to use the peaks as pointed knives to gut its prey. Only occasionally did the eagle's staring eye flash out from behind the thick fronds of something held tight in its beak: **a huge branch. A hundred strips of cowhide would not have sufficed to cover it.**

The portions that I have set in bold in this passage are taken from the *Mahabharata* (1.26.18–19), a great epic composed between 300 BCE and 300 CE. The standard translation of that passage, by J. A. B. van Buitenen, goes like this:

Penetrating that large mountainous enclave with his mind, the Bird [the eagle] swiftly flew to it with branch, tortoise, and elephant. A long leather strap cut from a hundred cowhides would have fallen short of girding the branch that the Bird carried in his flight.[1]

The rest is Calasso. So, too, in the rest of the book, Calasso rearranged passages from a rich variety of texts ranging from the oldest Indian text, the *Rig Veda* (c. 1500 BCE), to the medieval Puranas (c. 400 CE to 1400 CE). He wove them together so that they tell a single story of the creation of the earth and the gods, the quarrels of the god Shiva and his wife Parvati, and the destruction of the human race in the Armageddon of the great *Mahabharata* war. And he set this composite story against the background of the great rituals and the most vivid of the ancient Indian mystical meditations on the nature of reality (in the Upanishads, c. 600 BCE).

Calasso explains the title near the beginning of the book, when he tells us, translating a Vedic text (*Aitareya Brahamana* 3.21), how Ka got his name:

> The Creator god asked Indra, "Who (*ka* [the interrogative pronoun]) am I?" "Exactly what you said," said Indra. And in that moment, the Creator became Ka.

That is, the Creator said, "I am Who," and so he became Who. Indeed, later Hindu tradition, troubled by the open Vedic question, closed it by inventing a god whose name was Ka, Who, a passage that may have inspired the famous Abbott and Costello routine ("Who's on first?").

The book ends with a paragraph that takes us back to the beginning of the book, as the Indian apocalypse itself twists back to form a new beginning of creation:

---

1. J. A. B. van Buitenen, trans. and ed., *The Mahabharata*, (Chicago: University of Chicago Press, 1973), 7.

The watery expanse was endless in all directions. Only in one remote point could something be seen rising from it. Getting closer, you could make out a tree, but so thick and huge as to look like a mountain. Hidden among its branches, which formed an enameled pavilion, [the eagle] awoke [. . .] His eye settled on the very syllable from which everything had issued forth: Ka . . .

Ka, then, is the name of a god who is a question. It is also a word on the page of an English translation of an Italian translation of Hindu texts that reword and expand upon earlier Vedic texts.

The basic technique that makes this nested series of re-imaginations possible is very ancient and very Indian. Calasso finds what Hindu texts call the *bandhus*, the bonds, which he defines neatly as "the connections woven into all that is," the great themes that run like a golden thread through Hindu civilization. To find the bonds between the human body and the night sky, between the experience of pain and death and the performance of the Vedic sacrifice, is to find the meaning of it all. So, too, to find the bonds that link a brief riddle in the *Rig Veda* with a baroque story in the *Mahabharata*—and, beyond that, with the sensuous details of Calasso's personal imagination—is to make a kind of sense that no one before Calasso has even attempted to make. The *bandhus* that he uses to link the stories—bird, horse, snake, eye, tree, mountain, fire, water, death, the residue that survives the conflagration—are the same *bandhus* that Hindus have found in these texts for over two millennia. They are what Claude Lévi-Strauss called "mythemes," the recycled parts that the mythmaking handyman, the *bricoleur*, uses to restructure new stories out of old elements.[2]

Calasso is a consummate *bricoleur*. He even goes behind Hinduism to see the bond between Hinduism and Buddhism. He sees a *bandhu* between the

---

2. Claude Lévi-Strauss, "The Structural Study of Myth," in *Structural Anthropology*, trans. Claire Jacobson and Brooke Grundfest Schopef (Harmondworth, England: Penguin, 1963), 206–231.

very concept of the *bandhu* in Hinduism and the Buddhist concept of *prati-tyasamutpada*, usually translated as "the chain of dependent origination": "The unending net of the *bandhus,* of the `connections,` became a single lace [. . .] called *pratityasamutpada,* the interlinking of everything that arises." Calasso expands upon all of these bonds in the Hindu manner. The *Rg Veda* often sim-ply refers obliquely to a myth, which later Vedic texts such as the Brahmanas tell in a few stark sentences and the *Mahabharata* and Puranas spin out into hundreds of verses. Calasso describes this process: "From the allusive cipher of the *Rg Veda* and the abrupt, broken narratives of the Brahmanas, stories picked up only to be hurriedly dropped, one passed to the ruthless redun-dance of the Puranas, their incessant dilution, their indulgence in hypnotic and hypertrophic detail." And Calasso continues this process, imagining what the actors in the stark myth might have said in other, later genres, as if those actors had thought of the expanded ideas but somehow didn't get around to writing them down.

One aspect of this elasticity allows Hindu texts to build the commentar-ies right into the narrative, explaining the story even while they are telling it. Calasso brilliantly adapts this device to inform Western readers not only about matters that the Hindu commentaries discuss but also about matters that those commentaries neglect to mention, since they assume that their readers already know them. Thus he remarks of the building of a brick altar in the shape of a bird, "Here a false etymology, ever friend to thought, came to their aid. *Brick*, they said: *citi*. Bricks in layers. But what is *citi*? It's *cit*, which means `to think intensely.`"

Sometimes this expansion takes us beyond the Hindu commentaries and into the world of Western scholarship. After telling, in gorgeous physical and psychological detail, the story of the Indian Swan-Maiden, Urvasi, who mar-ries a human king and then abandons him when he violates his contract with her, Calasso remarks parenthetically on "the dispute between Vedic scholars, accustomed to arguing over every syllable: most of them understood Urvasi as meaning `you cannot possess me when I don't want you,` but Hoffmann, in his study on the injunctive tense, came to the conclusion that she had meant the opposite: `you can possess me even when I don't want you'; relationships between men and women have been marooned in this ambiguity ever since."

Purists (not I!) may feel that Calasso steps over the line on a few occasions, entirely out of the world of the text, even the world of its interpreters, and into the world not only of Western scholarship on India but also of Western fiction, as when he cryptically suggests that the god whose name is Ka "was to the gods as the K. of Kafka's *The Trial* and *The Castle* is to the characters of Tolstoy or Balzac." He adds these scraps of non-Indian texts to the scraps of myths, images, repeated cameo appearances of various gods, commentaries, and commentaries on commentaries. But ultimately he integrates them all into the continuous line of the narrative, drawing them all together in the same voice, his own voice.

This is a magnificent reading of Hindu texts. Its power arises in part simply through strong, vivid writing and Calasso's brilliant use of stunning, unexpected similes and metaphors. Thus the Creator, arranging the things that he will use in the ritual of creation, "looked like a beggar fussing with his few belongings," and the Creator's attachment to the things of existence remains "in the mind, buried in our being like a splinter no one can dislodge." When the gods wanted to create the avenging god Rudra, "like shrewd surgeons, they extracted the most ghastly shapes from inside themselves." The god Ganesha, "with his soft, young man's arms and wrinkly elephant's head with a broken tusk," is "like some toy left over from an earlier generation of children."

The immediacy of this language is well captured by Tim Parks's flowing English translation of Calasso's Italian translation of the Sanskrit. Parks has remarked that he thought of consulting English translations of the Sanskrit, until he realized that Calasso didn't translate the Sanskrit the way other people did, and it was Calasso that he had to translate, not the Sanskrit text. I have known the Sanskrit texts for over fifty years, but Calasso's fresh gaze makes me see things I never noticed before, such as the animality of the animal's experience in the story of the bird and the elephant, as well as many of the breathtakingly original connections, the *bandhus*. Is this an Indian book? An Italian book? An English book? All of the above.

One can use the different levels in different ways. The translation of the Ka episode ("I am Who"), for instance, is almost literal, and the exact source is listed in the appendix; the episode of the elephant and the tortoise (or turtle), by contrast, is richly expanded, translated with more license, more elegance, making it precious in the manner of Chapman's Homer, still beloved even when it has been technically superseded by more "accurate" translations. Still other parts of the book have the charm of Fitzgerald's version of Omar Khayyam: a thing of beauty, but far from the original, a masterpiece in its own right. And when you start putting Kafka into a Hindu text it is a translation only in the most generous postmodern terms. These last levels lack the authority of a quotable translation—the words cannot claim to represent the texts verbatim. But it touches down in the texts on every page.

When *Ka* was first published, I worried about the reception that it might have from its two audiences—experts on matters Indian and the general readers who have so enjoyed Calasso's other books. I worried that the very strength of the book, the way that it moves through different genres, might make it difficult for scholars to categorize and to decide just how authoritative a sourcebook it really is. And I worried that snobbery and the turf-guarding instincts of the closed academic shop might prevent scholars of Hindu mythology from using this as the basic introductory text that it so richly deserves to be. For Calasso is not a member of the Sanskrit Establishment.

My fears were only partially realized. In the twenty years since its publication, the book has not been widely adopted in the academic world as a reliable text, but it has found many passionate admirers and has been widely read and loved by students of Indian myth and religion and literature. As for the reaction of general readers, I feared that they might find the book too challenging, too disjointed, with too many different characters, different names. I feared that one reaction might be: too much Sanskrit! For indeed, perhaps out of a defensive desire to prove that he really does know the language, Calasso has put in more Sanskrit—diacriticals and all—than most card-carrying Sanskritists would do, inadvertently hauling into his text that thorny hedge as well as the treasure that he has stolen from behind it, and I worried that this might get in the way of the general reader.

In fact, I should not have worried. General readers have loved the book, Sanskrit and all, and reviewers in major newspapers and widely read journals have praised it to the skies. But when it comes to contemporary readers, I have a new fear. The past two decades have seen a revolution among Anglophone Indian readers of books about India. The rise of violently nationalist and fundamentalist Hindu politics, both in India and among Hindu diasporas in England and America, has led to a powerful resistance against what is presented as the inappropriate cultural appropriation of Hindu texts. The translation and/or interpretation of Sanskrit texts by non-Indian—more precisely, non-Hindu—Sanskritists has come to be seen as a kind of usurpation, a new form of colonization. In such a climate, there might well be new resistance to Calasso's brilliantly individualist internalization of the Hindu stories. This would be a terrible shame, for *Ka* is certainly the very best book about Hindu mythology that anyone, inside or outside of India, has ever written.

ELENA SBROJAVACCA

THE FOREST AND THE SNAKE

I would like to revisit certain places in the "Work in Progress" with the guidance of two images: the forest and the snake. Both are endowed with a symbolic meaning and are closely linked with the literary ideal that Calasso's work comes to delineate. Both are found, sometimes with their variants—in the case of the forest, the swamp, the thicket, and the woods; in the case of the snake, the dragon, Ouroboros, Ophiuchus, the Rod of Asclepius, and the caduceus of Hermes—in all of Calasso's books, and both can be traced back to similar fascinations.

The forest appears in *L'Impuro folle* (1974) in its wet and insalubrious version, the swamp. It seems to me these two natural realities may be said to belong to the same conceptual universe; they are spaces of indomitable nature, not cultivable and therefore extraneous to the aims of society. They can be approached as examples of vegetation that is both threatening, because it is wild, and sheltering, because it envelops. This inhospitable, dense, tangled nature is a perfect image of the psyche in its most enigmatic and frightening recesses. No wonder, in *L'Impuro folle*, there is a reference to the fear it inspires in the character of Freud. Pressed by President Schreber about the reasons for his terror, Freud replies:

> Only as a corpse could I get across the swamp unscathed—of course, I recognized her then, Mr. President, she was the gypsy *sitting on the swamp*, and around her were those other *squatters*: I was taken sidelong by an immense nostalgia, for the eternal feminine, immortal passion, but I knew that I couldn't stop, and that

the Etruscan tomb awaited me on the mountain. Temples can only be in swamps or on acropolis.[1]

The allusion here is to a passage in *The Interpretation of Dreams* in which the father of psychoanalysis reports an agonizing oneiric experience set in a swamp;[2] in Calasso's rewriting, the president becomes one of the inhabitants of the zone traversed in the dream. A primary element, already apparent in the source, is the connotation of the swamp as a locale of the feminine and hence of origins; similarly, in the analyses contained in the case study of Dora, the forest is associated with female genitalia, and here, too, the Nymphs are brought to bear.[3] Particularly packed with meaning is that final phrase, underlining the sacral destination of the swamp, the specular counterpart to the acropolis: for if the latter is the space of religious experience lived in a society with a solid ritual framework, the swamp is the place for religious experience lived in solitude, outside of a community context— the equivalent of what, in the Vedic vision, the forest is for the *sannyāsin*, the renunciant. In *The Ruin of Kasch*, it is precisely the chapter "The Forest Doctrine" that brings us back within the horizon of the Vedas, for which the forests are *aranya*, the "elsewhere" of the secret doctrine—the Āranyaka, the "books of the woods," which form the esoteric part of the *Brāhmana* and are destined to an anachoretic reading in the forest. These books contain lessons for initiates and so must be studied outside urban centers, far from the community.[4] Following this line of thought, Calasso writes: "The

---

1. Roberto Calasso, *L'impuro folle*, 75.
2. See Sigmund Freud, *The Interpretation of Dreams*, trans. A. A. Brill (Ware: Wordsworth Classics, 1997), 304.
3. "Now that we had 'nymphs' in the background of a 'dense forest' associated with it as well, there could be no doubt. We were looking at a symbolic sexual geography! The *nymphae*, as doctors but not laymen know—and not by any means all doctors—are the small labial folds in the female genitals, seen against the 'dense forest' of pubic hair." Sigmund Freud, *A Case of Hysteria (Dora)*, trans. Anthea Bell (Oxford University Press, 2013), 85.
4. See Oscar Botto, *Letterature antiche dell'India* (Milan: Casa Editrice Dr. Francesco Vallardi, Società Editrice Libraria, 1969), 37.

primordial world was suffocating, too dense, slimy. It was the bed of a cosmic swamp."[5] This place of indifferentiation was called Varuna: simultaneously an immense, coiled snake and the one who raised up the prop in the undifferentiated swamp, articulating that cosmic order (*rta*) which allows for life in all its manifestations. For Calasso, this metaphysical process is the backdrop to every story, divine and human.[6] Swamp and snake find themselves united in the cosmogonic moment.

Freud's difficult relationship with the swamp is also called into question in *The Ruin of Kasch*, in connection with the Austrian psychiatrist's inability to get to the bottom of some of his intuitions about the relationship between microcosm and macrocosm: the only element of contact between the individual and nature is identified by Freud in their shared "death drive." Even the passage quoted from *L'Impuro folle* seeks to highlight this conviction ("only as a corpse could I get across the swamp unscathed"), reinforcing the idea of a scholar trying to preserve the stability of his own conceptual framework. In the words of *Kasch*: "the most intolerable suspicion, for Freud, is that there might be a complicity between the outside world and the psyche: and yet he came across such complicity in the estuary where the waters of the unconscious mix with those of the world."[7] For Freud, to accept an interpenetration between the subject and the external world would mean falling "into the foul swamp in which the Ouroboros lives." The swamp is, then, associated with a particular image of a reptile coiled around the cosmos: the Ouroboros. This symbol of eternity and eternal return represents an "unfathomable" thought, which the modern man of science—of whom Freud is the prototype—is unable to accept.

The forest is thus a natural space that doesn't lend itself to being exploited as a reservoir of materials useful to technocratic and logocentric society, nor as a picturesque background in which man can find some diversion. The

---

5. Roberto Calasso, *The Ruin of Kasch*, 184.
6. *The Ruin of Kasch*, 185.
7. *The Ruin of Kasch*, 205.

forest, as we read in *Ka*, is also "the esoteric,"[8] the place of secret, initiatory knowledge. No wonder that the *Mahābhārata* begins in the forest, or that all the conversations of the *Purānas* are set in the forest. The woods is the place of choice for the acquisition of knowledge:

> "Forest" had never referred merely to the place that surrounds—how far?—the place where men live, but to the secret doctrine. To understand the world of men, and indeed every other world, one's point of observation must be out there in that harsh, dense realm where only animal voices were to be heard. It was the metaphysical place par excellence. He who thinks out in the forest is left entirely to himself: there he touches bottom, the baseline otherwise hidden beneath human chatter, there he goes back to being like a wild animal, which is the closest approximation to pure thought.[9]

The forest, understood as a physical, natural space, is the place to which the renunciants withdraw to lead a contemplative existence outside society. It will be said of them, in *The Unnamable Present*, that "when the forest is gone, they circulate in the streets like anyone else, but it's clear from a certain gleam in their eyes that they do not belong."[10] They are strangers to social life, like Nietzsche's Zarathustra, who seeks refuge in the forest after trying, in vain, to carry his message to the inhabitants of the city. The *sannyāsin*'s removal from the world was the final step in a natural evolution of the Vedic sacrifice, which eventually—in subsequent speculation—canceled itself out, while still firmly maintaining a sacrificial vision of the cosmos.[11] The modern individual, on the other hand, has been regarded since *The Ruin of Kasch* as a sort

---

8. Roberto Calasso, *Ka*, 202.
9. *Ka*, 355–56.
10. Calasso, *L'innominabile attuale*, 69.
11. See J. C. Heesterman, *The Broken World of Sacrifice: An Essay in an Ancient Indian Ritual* (Chicago: University of Chicago Press, 1993).

of degraded version of the renunciant, who has come back into the world ignorant of the previous evolutionary steps. Indeed, *homo saecularis* not only renounces the formal trappings of sacrifice, but denies its, so to speak, existential importance—denies, in other words, that the individual is a part of the cosmos, subject to a delicate balance of consumption and dispersion, and that every *surplus* must be dedicated to the powers that govern the whole. Having thus abandoned the rites, he will use the world (and nature) "in an unscrupulous and unprecedented way."[12]

At the same time, as the Freud episode demonstrates and as Calasso explains in *La Folie Baudelaire*, the forest is the unconscious; it is our overgrown mind, tangled and populated with strange presences.[13] "Kafka's world is a primordial forest," we read in *K.*; the reference is clearly directed at the psychic universe: "too fraught with strange noises and apparitions."[14] In the same volume, a long chapter dedicated to Kafka's relationship with the demons that torment his psyche includes one of the writer's diary entries:

> I enter the forest, find nothing and quickly, out of weakness, hurry back out; often, as I'm leaving the forest, I hear or think I hear the clanging of weapons from that battle. Perhaps the combatants are gazing through the forest darkness, looking for me, but I know so little about them, and that little is deceptive.[15]

A passage that elicits the following comment:

> If the forest, the *aranya*, is the place of esoteric knowledge, then the combatants are like the *rishis*, the sages who observe the world through the dark tangle of branches rather than from on high among

---

12. *The Ruin of Kasch*, 194.
13. See *La Folie Baudelaire*, 4.
14. *K.*, 3.
15. *K.*, 126

the stars of Ursa Major. Whoever ventures into the forest feels stalked by their gaze but can't manage to see them. And what has been passed down about them is by now very unreliable. Memory of names, of characters, is lost.[16]

The forest thus represents an interior space in which to encounter that divinity, that invisibility, which is the secret web of everything that exists. A web to which we are bound as much as any other creature, and to which the woods bears symbolic witness. In *La Folie Baudelaire*, we read that the poet always distinguished between two ways of understanding nature: the first was that of "*Correspondances*," that of a sacred, secret nature "whose presence most people never even notice";[17] the second was what his age exalted in the form of the idyll, the natural landscape as mere backdrop. Even so exceptional a reader of Baudelaire as Walter Benjamin did not accept this distinction, which he regarded as a "context of delusion." According to Calasso, this is because Benjamin, burdened by an Enlightenment inheritance, was in a certain sense frightened by the "abyss of myth." Because of his personal sensibility, all Benjamin could see in nature was a reflection of his own mental images. Against these, he wanted to oppose the force of a rationality that clarified and distinguished. He understood that Baudelaire's forest was the image of brute matter (as Aristotle had already conceived it), which precedes the forms of *logos* and is animated in the figures of myth, and he was at once attracted and disturbed:

> Like a child singing in the dark, Benjamin then wrote that precisely in that zone it was necessary to "penetrate, with the sharp ax of reason, and without looking to left or right, in order to avoid falling victim to the horror, which draws one from the depths of the forest." That exploration was never brought to a conclusion—and no

---

16. *K.*, 126.
17. *La Folie Baudelaire*, 18.

"sharp ax" would have served against what Benjamin described as "the brushwood of delirium and myth."[18]

In *The Celestial Hunter*, Calasso returns to the symbolic reach of wild nature as a location of original indistinctness, preceding and opposing every human society:

> Neither in the *pólis* nor in the village nor in the palace did people play around with what preceded every *pólis*, every village, every palace. One day, that precedent would be called nature. But in the beginning it showed itself only as a forest, an undomesticated, untouched place. And there a life unfolded parallel to that of the community.[19]

The forest has a home in the eternity of myth as an imaginal background, where the great rupture between the individual and the cosmos, between man and nature, takes place. It is precisely there that the hunter's activity begins:

> If all that takes place in myth then repeats itself in history, the birth of the individual took place in a forest, when the hunter appeared there. He was the first self-sufficient being, who has no need to be in dialogue, except with his art. His is the first solitary profile, aloof from every tribe, that comes to meet us in nature. In the background: animals and plants.[20]

Accepting the idea of a deep contract with nature puts man in an awkward situation, forcing him to confront that moment in his own evolutionary history when he wanted to get the best of the animal by imitating it and upset a universal balance by transforming himself into a predator. Man has a constant

---

18. *La Folie Baudelaire*, 19.
19. *Il Cacciatore Celeste*, 63.
20. *Il Cacciatore*, 64.

need, aggravated by his original guilt, to differentiate himself, to feel that the animal is something other than he is, to annul that earlier communion. Calasso establishes an equivalence between the hunter of a traditional society and the modern *homo saecularis*. For both, confronting the forest means coming face to face with the original guilt, venturing into a space—physical or mental, or physical and mental—where one is never alone. It means feeling lost and surrounded:

> It was difficult to break free from the hunt. Like the woman's body upon the man, the forest left an odorous trail upon the hunter. Thus some chewed on alder bark, to keep the disease of the forest from contaminating them [. . .] Whoever has crossed or continues to cross the border with the invisible—even and especially if the invisible is not recognized as such—will live in the state of those who, at any moment, expect to be attacked. And he knows very well where the attack will come from—even if sometimes he is the only one who knows.[21]

The forest is a state of consciousness, a place that can only be accessed by those who accept the risk of getting lost in their own tangled interior vegetation. And so the forest is also an existential choice, sometimes conscious, sometimes almost obligatory. In ancient India, there was a place for the person who embarked on a path of solitude and contemplation, situating himself outside of society; within the context of ritual time, his position had a meaning, a recognized role. In the contemporary secular world, from a certain point of view, we are all renunciants. On a global level, we have indeed broken free from the liturgical bond of sacrifice. We believe we are total strangers to it, yet nevertheless we remain linked, according to Calasso, to the existential node that sacrifice represents. Who, then, is the true renunciant today? Who is the new

---

21. *Il Cacciatore*, 34.

anchorite, unfettered from any social bond and, at the same time, somehow aware of the need to reckon with the Residue? Here is the answer *Ardor* gives:

> Several thousand years later, with whom would we now associate this figure? With all those who are driven by a powerful urge—they often prefer not to call it duty, but it is certainly something they feel obliged to do for someone, someone they may never know—and they concentrate their energies on some form of composition, which in turn is offered to someone unknown. They are the artists, those who study. They all find the origin and purpose of what they do in the practice of their art, in their studies. They are Flaubert, who roars in the solitude of his room at Croisset. Without asking for what reason and for what purpose. But absorbed in working out ardor, *tapas*, in a form.[22]

The forest is a place where the soul is filled with fear, because it is the site of the unknown. In *The Unnamable Present*, we read of the "inclination to expose oneself to the shock of the unknown" as "a secret and precious sensation, which says a great deal about the quality of a person," and of an "archaic remnant" which is ineradicable. Indeed, it is precisely the writers—a "lean sect," as Calasso calls them[23]—who don't renounce venturing out, aware of the good they can find there:

> they know that it's an irreplaceable sensation, and a prerequisite for any connection with the past. That feeling is like the first phase of an initiation rite, which takes place in darkness and silence. But it is indispensible to establishing a relationship with the unknown.[24]

---

22. *Ardor*, 221.
23. *L'innominabile attuale*, 88.
24. *L'innominabile attuale*, 88.

Going back in time, at the outset of the "work in progress," we find a perfectly coherent image. In *The Ruin of Kasch*, the forest is in fact inhabited by those who, not yielding to the dictatorship of the ego, worship the "sudden forces" that rule over the subject:

> A woodland of death, similar to that lugubrious surrounding of myrtle and cypress described by Virgil (*Secreti celant calles . . .*), grim abode of suicides, where in silence, many of those dear to us succumbed, gazing scornfully, like Dido, at prudent Aeneas, who did not mention the Ego, but had wrapped it into a safe bundle (*atque inimica refugit in nemus umbriferum*). What could have called you to that obscurity, apart from the attraction of a detail, of an obstinate, unspeakable singularity, around which you enjoyed wandering, into which you went, stubborn guardians, like marmots among their rough stones? Whoever was led to that life was devoted from the very beginning to the discontinuous, hostile to all *aequalitas*, observer (worshipper?) of sudden forces, incapable of a long breath that envelops every part.[25]

In *Kasch*, it is, moreover, clearly stated that the forest, from the Romantics on, is the place where the only sacrificial function still granted is performed—the function with which is invested the artist:

> in the absence of a ritual, of an order, the only role left is that of the victim, who wanders the forest, prey to Rudra, waiting for his fatal arrows. This is the consumption that kills Novalis and Keats. For Hölderlin, Rudra is Apollo, who strikes him down in Bordeaux. When, with Rimbaud, the writer becomes officially *maudit*, it is already time for a change, time to go selling weapons in Harar. The

---

25. *The Ruin of Kasch*, 339.

victim discovers sadly that the world has already prepared an archaic niche for him. He must now return to the forest. In the city, he will be anonymous, barely visible, he will write business letters in English, he will sit in a café after office hours: the forest is Pessoa's trunk, crammed full of names.[26]

The snake, too, is intrinsically linked to literature: the famous episode in Genesis suffices to demonstrate its ability to give rise to stories. Traditionally, the most disparate traits have been attributed to this animal: in the Christian world, these range from the malevolent subtlety corroborated by the first book of the Pentateuch to the caution recommended by Jesus in the Gospel of Matthew ("be ye wise as serpents and harmless as doves"[27]); if one turns to the Greek world, one goes from the omniscience recognized by the Gnostics, who believed the snake to be the author of the divine gnosis (represented by Phanes encircled by a nimbus), to the dynamic awakening of the forces of Hermes's caduceus, or the salvific power of Asclepius's rod. The snake can, in short, be considered the symbolic animal par excellence. It is not surprising, then, that the "work in progress," in which so much space is given over to reflections on modes of substitution, makes extensive use of this image. A symbol, according to *The Ruin of Kasch*,

> reveals the interpenetration, the indissoluble superimposition of things: symbol is a specter that enters another specter, mingles with it, merges into it, disappears. The symbol drags behind it, as a *catena aurea*, all that it has crossed.[28]

It is interesting to consider that, in addition to filling his literary work with snakes, Calasso refers us to the reptile to describe his own publishing

---

26. *The Ruin of Kasch*, 180.
27. Matthew 10:16.
28. *The Ruin of Kasch*, 229.

company. In an essay published in *Cento lettere a uno sconosciuto*, in fact, we find a fundamental starting point for coming to terms with the Adelphi project: "what is a publishing house if not a long serpent of books?"[29] The serpent is here an image of ideal continuum: the correlation is with its characteristic epidermis, composed of different scales which form a single fabric; in the same way, Adelphi, for all the variegatedness of its published offerings, is for Calasso a single skin, an organic whole.

What one discovers in the Calassian universe is the same thing the writer discovered in the work of Giambattista Tiepolo: "wherever you turn, you will find that snake. And it is the only species of ascertainable universality: aesthetic, enigmatic."[30] In a television interview, Calasso acknowledged the animal's relevance to his own work: "the snake appears in all my books and is an emissary of the continuum."[31] In this way, he gave an important hint: one must see in the snake a sign of the continuous within the discrete. The animal's presence should force us to look at the manifestations of the discrete from a cosmic point of view.

The snake is connected with a whole series of cosmogonic images in the "work in progress." In addition to that of Varuna, there also appears the image—important to the Gnostic tradition—of the copulation between Time Without Age and Ananke. We are told, in *The Marriage of Cadmus and Harmony*, how the two deities, coupling as snakes, generated from their interwoven bodies Phanes, the Protogonos.[32] In this story, the snake is, in the first place, a separation from the continuum. Again, as with the forest or the swamp, we find ourselves confronted with an image of origin as indifferentiation. The snake is the first articulation that upsets the original balance, and makes existence possible. It is the image of a fracture—of a necessary

29. *Cento lettere a uno sconosciuto*, 20.
30. *Tiepolo Pink*, 237.
31. See "Eco della storia incontra Roberto Calasso", intervista di Gianni Riotta, *Eco della Storia*, Rai Cultura, 16 luglio, 2016, 37'15".
32. *The Marriage of Cadmus and Harmony*, 200.

tearing of the continuum. The ultimate metamorphic animal, owing to its ability to change its skin, it is an ideal emblem of the passage from one state to another, the transition from one mode of being to another. In the continuum that is the primordial cosmos, the snake is existence as manifestation (Phanes, from *phainomai*) and therefore also a rupture in what *was* invisible. In the discontinuum, which is the world following the originary manifestation, the serpent is a memory of the continuum. *The Marriage of Cadmus and Harmony* recounts how Zeus, who had swallowed Phanes in order to become lord of the gods, rapes his mother Rhea Demeter in the form of a snake, playing out again with her the interweaving of Time Without Age and Ananke:

> But why did the god decide to make that particular knot [a Heracleotic knot] to rape his mother? Zeus was remembering something and wanted to repeat it. Just as men would one day recall a divine precedent in everything they did, so Zeus recalled those gods before the gods whom he had been able to contemplate when he swallowed Phanes and all his powers.[33]

The same knot is found on Hermes's caduceus, to remind us how delicate and uncertain the balance is between good and evil, which the snake, as an emissary of the continuous within the discontinuous, contains. In *La Folie Baudelaire*, Phanes returns in the role of the monstrous being that the poet encounters in his dream of an enigmatic brothel-museum. The solitary inhabitant of this house of ill repute is compared by Calasso to an ancient statue enshrined in Mérida. If modernity is no longer able to deal with the continuum, its representative with the serpentine tail can only live imprisoned in a museum, rendered harmless by his position on the margins of society:

---

33. *The Marriage of Cadmus and Harmony*, 203.

In the epoch of *Le Siècle*, which endures to this day, Phanes still exists, but he is denied the honor of being a statue. Now he is someone who "has lived," a freak on show alongside images of other freaks, a "monster born in the house" (of prostitution), from which he has probably never gone out. He is no longer the one who bears up the world, but someone whom the world keeps imprisoned in the remotest part of himself.[34]

The snake is linked, too, to numerous theogonic events, and its cyclical return in the divine stories is also proof of the recursivity of time, agitated by the "demon of repetition"[35]: Zeus and Rhea Demeter take the form of snakes, and from them Persephone is born; by coupling with Persephone in the form of a snake, Zeus gives life to Dionysus Zagreus; by conjoining with Semele in the same form, he gives rise to Dionysus:

From snake to snake the world went on propagating itself in era after era. Every time Zeus transformed himself into a snake, time's arrow flew backward, to bury itself in the origin of things. At which the world seemed to hold its breath, listening for that backward movement that marks the passage from one era to another. And so it was when, from the union of Zeus and Rhea Demeter in the form of snakes, Persephone was born, "the girl whose name cannot be uttered," the unique girl to whom Zeus would transmit the secret of the snake.[36]

The Marriage of Cadmus and Harmony, a book dedicated to things that "are always,"[37] cannot but overflow with snakes. These reptiles return, in one chapter after another, to mark important nexus in Calasso's personal

---

34. *La Folie Baudelaire*, 152.
35. See Nietzsche's *The Gay Science*.
36. *The Marriage of Cadmus and Harmony*, 204.
37. See the epigraph to *The Marriage of Cadmus and Harmony*: "These things never happened, but always are" (Saloustios, *Of Gods and of the World*).

theogony: Cadmus kills the snake of Ares; Aphrodite makes a gift to Harmony of a necklace of snakes; Cadmus and Harmony, setting off on a chariot in the final scene of the book, twine their hair together like snakes.

In *The Marriage*, the snake often appears opposite the bull, another animal dear to Zeus and connected with storytelling (we think of the stories told by the cave paintings), with feral, monstrous indomitability (we think of the Minotaur), and with the hatred of Apollo—who sent Theseus to kill the Cretan monster, while he himself killed Python—but the bull is also linked with earth and fire (in the form of sacrificial offerings), whereas the snake belongs to the waters.

Images of the snake appear as early as *L'Impuro Folle*. Both through Tiresia's daughter, Manto, the serpentine-haired girl who carries on talking with Schreber,[38] and, more significantly, with the mention of the myth of Apollo and Python. In one of the monologues that stud the novel in fact, the president speaks of "Apollo the Oblique [. . .] jealous of the lazy dragon lady coiled up at Delphi, who knew the future's signs."[39] The story of the triumphant Apollo, who kills Python to take possession of the spring Telphusa, is indeed so rooted in the Calassian imaginary that it resurfaces constantly in the most disparate places in his oeuvre, beginning with the first book. The same myth is rehearsed in *Literature and the Gods* and in *La Follia che viene dalle Ninfe*. It is therefore evident that the snake—the animal that creeps, slithering, into every crevice—is linked with the Nymphs, and so also with possession and divine enthusiasm. In this regard, *The Marriage of Cadmus and Harmony* remembers: "*Théos*, the indeterminate divine, was an invasion, of body and mind. It was our becoming intimate with what is most alien. And nothing is more alien than the snake."[40]

In the story of Apollo and Telphousa, it is the animal that suffers violence by submitting to the brutality with which the divine can manifest itself. The snake is associated with the waters—the springs—and linked with the images

---

38. *L'impuro folle*, 108.
39. *L'impuro folle*, 110.
40. *The Marriage of Cadmus and Harmony*, 206.

that emerge from the waters, like the Nymphs (Python *in primis*), and, in general, with all mental phantasms. It is a representative of the continuous production of images to which our brain is prone:

> In every story, if you go back, as far back as you can, to the point where every horizon disappears, you find a snake, the tree, water. It's either a snake that covers a spring of water with its coils or a lump, a knot drifting on the waters, a circular cushion bearing a divine figure as it slithers across the waves. Or a snake coiled around a trunk growing out of the water. And you can also find all this by looking inside yourself, as the *Kattha Upanishad* claims some people did long ago ("a certain wise man who was seeking immortality looked inside himself by turning the globes of his eyes back to front"). The snake is coiled around the trunk from which the essence, the *rasa*, dribbles down, just as the Twisted Goddess, Devī Kundalinī, wraps her coils three and a half times around the *susumnā*, the vertical stream that crosses the *meru*, the spine, but also Mount Meru, emerging below the vault of the skull or the cosmos, where Śiva on his lotus throne awaits the awakening call.[41]

The snake is thus also an inhabitant of our psyche; it is linked with the water holes of the Nymphs and with mental images. The story of Apollo and Python demonstrates that the metamorphic knowledge of the Nymph, the knowledge of divination, can be twisted to suit the wishes of a god who has no familiarity with the waters or springs, but who knows how to bend the Nymphs to his will: Apollo, god of order and meter, must kill the snake in order to appropriate that kind of knowledge. In *The Marriage*, the story of Apollo and Python is called " the model for killing monsters." In *Ka*, it is compared to the more ancient myth of Indra and Vrtra. By spearing him through,

---

41. *Ka*, 336–37.

Indra kills the snake Vrtra (from the root *vr* = to compel, to captivate), a constrictor that contained the waters; Apollo is thus a "Western cousin" of the Indra who "loosed his arrow at Python, coiled up like Vrtra on the mountain at Delphi."[42] The killing of Vrtra also involved the liberation of the Soma, whch in the Vedic tradition was a king and, at the same time, an intoxicating substance guarded by a Nymph-Snake. The gist of both stories, according to the author of *Ka*, is the same: "no one who aspires to sovereignty can achieve his goal except by means of the Snake and the Nymph."[43] The snake is a monstrous being with whom the hero must go head to head: a danger that, once confronted, leads to a reward of much larger scope. That is why, in *The Ruin of Kasch*, Indra's murder is called " the archetype of every dragon-killing,"[44] which is to say the archetype of every encounter between a hero and a monster. In *The Celestial Hunter*, Python is said to be only "the last survivor of an age of monsters."[45] A mythic age, with ephemeral boundaries, in which every contrast was motivated by a higher necessity; a time when every duel was a metamorphosis that left an indelible trace of the monster on the hero: the Sphinx on Oedipus, the Minotaur on Theseus:

> But to see the labyrinth from outside, and to kill it in the figure of the Minotaur, one must have penetrated as far as its center, which is the mouth from which one goes out into the space of isolated, separate things, arranged in a precarious manner: the space where the sacrifice must constantly weave an airy connection, between emptiness and emptiness. The hero who kills and at the same time is born is in danger of losing contact with his cosmic victim, with his enemy who is also the source of all power: with water.[46]

---

42. *Ka*, 248.
43. *Ka*, 253.
44. *The Ruin of Kasch*, 185.
45. *Il Cacciatore Celeste*, 214.
46. *The Ruin of Kasch*, 185–86.

The snake is the perfect representative of this complex balancing of forces. Considered in almost every culture to be an ambivalent being, it symbolizes the continuous in the "work in progress." Every time it appears, according to Calasso, it ideally forces us to return to that primordial state, indefinite and inarticulate, from which it has detached itself in order to give life to all. Humanity lives in discontinuity, in articulation; in the great cosmic web, the mind can catch only bits and pieces, illuminating only modest portions of reality. Although it belongs to the continuous, in fact it needs to operate in the discrete. The snake is an image of extraordinary power that reminds humanity where it came from:

> The deeper you go into stories about snakes in ancient Greece, the more pointless—and inapplicable—becomes the usual division between *benign* and *malign*. The snake obviously transcends this— indeed it is the emblem of that which generally transcends this opposition. The serpent is power, in its undifferentiated and indistinct state. Or at least in that state that seems undifferentiated and indistinct to our eyes, when we draw near it and discover it, in uncertainty and terror. As a permanent reminder of that state, the snake creeps into every story and over every body. The divine is that which has not lost contact with the serpent. Which may even kill it or condemn it, but recognizes it. And sometimes may use it as an ally or an accomplice.[47]

The divine, which is the continuous and the invisible, is in various ways linked to the serpent. In *Tiepolo Pink*, Calasso makes reference to the snake of Genesis and notes how, following his instructions, Eve first observes the fruit of the tree of knowledge and discovers it is "good for food and pleasing to the eye."[48] He argues:

---

47. *Tiepolo Pink*, 165.
48. Genesis, 3:6.

There is therefore a very close connection between the act of looking and the animal that is "more subtle than any beast of the field."
Wherever we deal with images, we encounter the serpent. Or a trace
of the serpent.[49]

The reason Giambattista Tiepolo sought to fill his works with snakes,
then, had to do with obedience, conscious or not, to his own iconolatry—for
Calasso, the only form of submission to which a modern artist must adapt.
The images are connected with another famous biblical episode linked to the
serpent, also summoned up in *La Follia che viene dalla Ninfe*. The story's protagonist is Moses, who in the Book of Numbers finds himself crossing the des-
ert, leading his people, who are more and more exhausted and malnourished.
The Israelites begin to despair of their chances for survival, and they complain
to Moses about God's plans. The Lord, angered, sends forth snakes which bite
and kill the people in great number. The Israelites then rush to plead for God's
mercy through Moses. Jahweh orders the Prophet to brandish a pole topped
with a serpent of brass, saying to whoever had been bitten to look upon it, and
that whoever would look upon it would be saved:

> Moses's gesture, when he brandished a bronze serpent and told the
> murmuring Jews to *look at it*, was a gesture that marked the discov-
> ery that evil can be cured by its image. Indeed that evil can be cured
> *only* by the contemplation of its image. Around, there is nothing else
> but sand and snakes hidden in the sand. Yet Moses ordered all to
> contemplate an object very similar to the amulets that proliferated in
> Egypt. But where did it spring from? There was no forge, no metals.
> Yet the command worked. It was one of the most crucial discoveries
> that can be made. A silent discovery this time. Not etched on a plate,
> nor found in a text. It was the discovery of the image, of its healing

---

49. *Tiepolo Pink*, 171.

power. It is one of the supreme Jewish paradoxes that this discovery was made by he who would be remembered and celebrated as the enemy of images.[50]

For this reason, an "esoteric" work such as that of Giambattista Tiepolo turns out to be full of the mysterious apparitions of snakes. Only Tiepolo could, according to Calasso, indicate the path that, in the Age of Reason, an artist must follow in order to arrive at the only kind of revelation granted to secular humanity—the revelation of Form:

> there, unbeknownst to all and fixed only by a vibrant and febrile metallic point, an ancient pact would continue to be renewed, tightening into a knot that was the "*nodus et copula mundi*," as Ficino put it. A knot assimilable to that formed by the snakes coiled around wooden staves, loyal guardians of the place."[51]

We can see the same knot inside our mind—which belongs to the original continuum—but only through fleeting illuminations. This is for Calasso the rather heroic mission of literature in the modern world: to seek contact with that primordial state and to bear witness to it, entering the most mysterious and dangerous recesses of the psyche, equipped with Apollo's bow and his formal rigor. With these weapons alone, the writer will be able to kill the snake and take possession of its knowledge, or, more humanely, he may look at it, speak of it, and hope for salvation.

Translated from the Italian by Alex Andriesse

---

50. *Tiepolo Pink*, 172.
51. *Tiepolo Pink*, 88.

CHARLES SIMIC

PARADISE LOST[1]

> "Everything, in the world, exists to end up in a book."
> —Mallarmé

The surprising durability of ancient Greek myths in an age when Homer, Ovid, and other classics are no longer taught in our schools is astonishing and not easy to explain. In this country, we have never been very good at history, barely troubling to remember our own in much detail, and the same is true of the literary past, which is gradually being expunged from the curriculum. When it comes to pagan myth, most of the champions of progress take it for granted that they have nothing to say to us anymore. How wrong they are. This year, for example, saw the publication of *Gods and Mortals*, an anthology of modern poems based on classical myths.[2] Out of 323 poems in the book, roughly one fourth are the work of contemporary American poets. When it comes to being out of sync with reigning intellectual fashions, poets get the prize every time.

As for the anthology itself, the structure is thematic, so one finds poems on almost every figure in mythology, with Orpheus and Eurydice and the wanderings and homecoming of Odysseus seeming to be the favorites. Poets who have vastly different and frequently unreconcilable ideas of poetry, such as, for example, Joseph Brodsky and Gregory Corso, Robert Creeley and Richard Wilbur, Lucille Clifton and Jorie Graham, are to be

---

1. Originally published in *The New York Review of Books*, September 20, 2001. Reprinted with permission of the author.
2. *Gods and Mortals: Modern Poems on Classical Myths*, edited by Nina Kossman (Oxford University Press, 2001).

found reflecting on some god or mortal hero. To paraphrase Charles Olson, myth is a bed in which human beings continue to make love to the gods.

What is it in these stories that the poets find indispensable? The answer has to be that they still feed their imagination. What Ezra Pound said long ago still appears to be true today: "No apter metaphor having been found for certain emotional colors, I assert that gods exist." Here's a poem of his from 1912 commemorating that discovery:

THE RETURN

See, they return; ah, see the tentative
Movements, and the slow feet,
The trouble in the pace and the uncertain
Wavering!
See, they return, one, and by one,
With fear, as half-awakened;
As if the snow should hesitate
And murmur in the wind,
and half turn back;
These were the "Wing'd-with-Awe,"
Inviolable,
Gods of the wingèd shoe!
With them the silver hounds,
sniffing the trace of air!
Haie! Haie!
These were the swift to harry;
These the keen-scented;
These were the souls of blood.
Slow on the leash,
pallid the leash-men!

Even in our days of technology and globalization, it may be that the world we live in is too complex a place to explain with just one god. We need Eros, Apollo, Dionysus, Narcissus, and the rest of their tribe to make sense of things. For poets, there is also an additional motive. The big headache for over a hundred years has been how to find a larger setting for one's personal experience. Without some sort of common belief, theology, mythology—or what have you—how was one supposed to figure out what it all means? The only option remaining, or so it seemed, was for each one of us to start from scratch and construct our own cosmology as we lay in bed at night. A poet who backtracks into myth is longing for a community that no longer exists. Or if it still does, it is a community of solitary readers and insomniac philosophers who are unknown to one another.

The Italian writer Roberto Calasso's new book of essays, *Literature and the Gods*, based on Weidenfeld Lectures he gave at Oxford, takes up this very subject of what we mean when we talk about gods. It discusses such figures as Hölderlin, Baudelaire, Nietzsche, Nabokov, Leopardi, Lautréamont, and Mallarmé and makes keen observations on several others. What is startling about his brief survey of the renewed interest in myth and pagan deities in Western literature is how recent it is in some countries. In eighteenth-century France, Greek myths were called childish fables, Shakespeare was seen as barbaric, and biblical tales were regarded as nothing more than priestly indoctrination to suffocate any potentially free spirit and enlightened mind. While the gods were never entirely lost sight of, supplying a bit of rhetorical dazzle and moral allegory in occasional poems and plays, only in painting, Calasso argues, did they run free over the centuries:

> Thanks to its wordless nature, which allows it to be immoral without coming out and saying as much, the painted image was able to restore the gods to their glamorous and terrifying apparitions as simulacra. Hence a long and uninterrupted *banquet of the gods* runs parallel with Western history from Botticelli and Giovanni Bellini,

through Guido Reni and Bernini, Poussin and Rembrandt (*The Rape of Persephone* would itself suffice), Saraceni and Furini and Dossi, right through to Tiepolo.

With the Romantics, the world of the Greeks returns as a lost paradise and an aesthetic ideal. Speaking about gods became acceptable again. There's hardly a European poet in the nineteenth century who did not mention them. Their reasons were often superficial: they wanted to sound noble, exotic, pagan, erotic, erudite, or poetic. According to Calasso, the attraction of these antique fables for someone like Leopardi is that they were the mysterious remnants of a world where reason hadn't yet been able to unleash the full effects of its lethal power, "a power that 'renders all objects to which it turns its attention small and vile and empty, destroys the great and the beautiful and even, as it were, existence itself.'"

This attitude, as Leopardi himself realized, was absurd. Pretending to be ancient Romans or Greeks while concealing the fact that they were modern Europeans made some of the poets look silly. In France, among the Parnassians and Symbolists, that silliness had a use: it sheltered one against the vulgarity of the shopkeeper. "Everything can be at home in this century but poetry," Leopardi wrote, a sentiment far removed from what Emerson and Whitman were saying a few years later; for them, in America at least, this was the golden age for poets.

"Difficult are the gods for men to see," the ancient *Hymn to Demeter* already complains. Before they became literary clichés, the pagan deities lived the quiet lives of exiles in our midst, revealing their true nature only to a select few. The more modern literature tried to be absolutely original, the more it rummaged in the unconscious, the more it came face to face with them. Once again Orpheus picked up his lute, Venus seduced mortal men, Sisyphus shouldered his rock, and Odysseus dallied with Calypso. As Calasso points out—and there's no disputing him—perhaps only to Hölderlin among the poets did the gods show themselves in their full radiance. Yet their supreme mystery has always been close. "Whatever else it might be, the divine is certainly the thing that imposes with maximum intensity the sensation of being alive," Calasso writes. Where we find ourselves fully awake, divinities make their appearance. Emily Dickinson used the word "awe" to describe that experience in which the entire familiar world loses its normal significance and leaves one speechless in the presence of something one can no longer name. For us moderns, these cannot be the same gods as of old. Calasso writes:

> They are no longer made up of just the one family, however complicated, residing in their vast homes on the slopes of a single mountain. No, now they are multitudes, a teeming crowd in an endless metropolis. It hardly matters that their names are often exotic and unpronounceable, like the names one reads on the doorbells of families of immigrants. The power of their stories is still at work. Yet there is something new and unusual about the situation: this composite tribe of gods now lives *only* in its stories and scattered idols. The way of cult and ritual is barred, either because there is no longer a group of devotees who carry out the ritual gestures, or because even when someone does perform these gestures they stop short. The statues of Shiva and Vishnu still drip with offerings, but Varuna is a remote and shapeless entity to the Indian of today, while Prajapati is only to be found in books. [Varuna was the supreme lord of the cosmos, the keeper of divine order. Prajapati was the lord of creation.] And this, one might say, has become the natural condition of the gods: to appear in books—and often in books that few will ever open. Is this the prelude to extinction? Only to the superficial observer. For in the meantime all the powers of the cult of the gods have migrated into a single, immobile and solitary act: that of reading.

The effect of such solitary acts of piety and devotion of the few, as Calasso has amply shown, ought not to be underestimated. Two of his previously translated books, *The Marriage of Cadmus and Harmony* (1993) and *Ka* (1998), are for-midably ambitious attempts to retell the stories of Greek and Indian mythology, untangle their many variants, and meditate on their meaning. "Stories," he writes about the Greeks, "never live alone: they are the branches of a family that we have to trace back, and forward." It is the same with India. "So many things happening, so many stories one inside the other, with every link hiding yet more stories." Calasso serves as our guide in the maze.

Both of these books have been extravagantly praised, and deservedly so. In the ambition of the undertaking and wealth of material, they are comparable to Ovid's *Metamorphoses* or *The Thousand and One Nights*, except the end result is very different. What Calasso has done is original and difficult to classify. The stories not only reassemble the ancient myths into a new synthesis, but they include literary, philosophical, and historical commentary. Still, despite their extraordinary erudition and insight into the minds of these two cultures, these are not scholarly studies. They are powerful works of the imagination in their own right that will most likely inspire future generations of mythographers and poets.

Calasso refreshes our memory of how violent the myths are. Murder, rape, incest, and acts of unbelievable cruelty are matters of course. It is a world in which the innocents suffer, justice is infrequent, and when it does come, it often comes too late. The trouble with too many poems on classical myths is that they are often no more than a pretext for lyric posturing, an evocation of the beauty of the bygone world and its ill-fated heroes and heroines at the expense of the harsher vision of the original. The perennial challenge in recounting myth, it seems to me, is how to make believable a pretty girl who is half fish and whose song mesmerizes sailors.

•

Calasso is a consummate storyteller, mixing drama, gossip, and even passages of poetry. He brings to life the ancient soap operas with their large cast of divine and human characters and keeps us entertained. Like all good stories and poems, the myths have many layers of meaning, which Calasso's cunningly told narratives manage to preserve. Did ideas come first and the myths came afterward in order to illustrate them, or did the Greeks discover them as they listened to the stories? Here is an example of what I have in mind, from Calasso's recreation of the myth of Persephone, the goddess of fertility who was carried off into the underworld by Hades (Pluto). In the Eleusinian mysteries she appears under the name Kore:

> It was a place where dogs would lose their quarry's trail, so violent was the scent of the flowers. A stream cut deep through the grass of a meadow that rose at the edge to fall sheer in a rocky ravine into the very navel of Sicily. And here, near Henna, Kore was carried off. When the earth split open and Hades' chariot appeared, drawn by four horses abreast, Kore was looking at a narcissus. She was looking at the act of looking. She was about to pick it. And, at that very moment, she was herself plucked away by the invisible toward the invisible.

What fascinates Calasso is that moment of heightened consciousness. Kore sees herself reaching for a narcissus, just as Hades snatches her away to be his bride. Interestingly, Calasso writes that her name doesn't just mean "girl" but "pupil" of the eyes. In the myth she turns away from the beautiful flower, their eyes meet, and she sees her pupil reflected in his. If as Socrates claims, and Calasso points out, the Delphic maxim "Know Thyself" can be understood as "Look at Thyself," this marvelous story of the double gaze conveys a magnificent insight. As our consciousness divides to observe itself—observation for which looking at a narcissus is an evident metaphor—that invisible other watching within us is no other than our death, as it were. In other words, and this strikes me as both true and astonishing, we come to our self-knowledge through the eye of our mortality since, obviously, if we were going to be around forever such experiences would not be so precious.

The Greeks, as Calasso demonstrates, had more in mind. For them, this moment is not just about self-knowledge but is also about aesthetics. Our precarious life, fleeting and irreplaceable, has another dimension. That which exists once and only once is beautiful, the myths keep telling us. It is precisely because we are mortal beings that things have a significance and an intense presence at times. To come to understand that was a momentous discovery for literature. What has lyric poetry been for almost three thousand years, one can ask, but an aesthetic justification of mortality?

"The first enemy of the aesthetic was meaning," Calasso writes in *The Marriage of Cadmus and Harmony*. In the aesthetic experience the meaning is there, but it doesn't impose itself. What dominates is a presence of someone or something one does not wish to name just then. The search for meaning takes one away from what is there before one's eyes. Once again, Calasso is calling attention to the moment of heightened consciousness, its self-sufficiency and the wordless understanding that comes with it. Like a "pure light of midsummer," such is the presence of the god Dionysus according to the poet Pindar. Perfection always keeps something hidden, says Calasso. And to conceal with light was always the Greeks' specialty.

•

If our own classic myths still resonate imaginatively and philosophically for us, what about the ones from India? At first reading *Ka*, one is overwhelmed by the unfamiliarity of the names, the oddness of the stories and their endlessly metamorphosing divinities. We are likely to be baffled by the plurality of viewpoints, clashing metaphysical ideas, and the difficulty of drawing a distinction between different traditions and schools of thought. Once again, Calasso's prose, in Tim Parks's masterful translation, casts its narrative spell.

Eventually one begins to situate oneself in an exotic universe. As in Greece, the enigma of consciousness—that light capable of seeing what it illuminates— is at the center of cosmic mystery, as it was understood by the Aryans (or Aryas) who invaded India around 1500 BC:

> Just as some claim that every true philosopher thinks but one thought, the same can be said of a civilization: from the beginning the Aåøryas thought, and India has ever continued to think, the thought that dazzled us *r.s.is*: the simple fact of being conscious. There is not a shape, not an event, not an individual in its history that cannot, in a certain number of steps, be taken back to that thought, just as Yaåøjñavlkya demonstrated that the three thousand, three hundred and six gods could all be taken back to a single word: *brahman*.

Here is an Indian myth that reads like a sequel to the Greek one about Kore and Hades:

> The Person in the Eye is not born alone, cannot exist alone. The first couple were the two Persons in the Eye. In the right eye was Death. In the left eye his companion. Or again: in the right eye was Indra [the warrior god and thunder god of the Vedas]. In the left eye his partner Indrani. It was for these two that the gods made that division between the eyes: the nose. Behind the barrier of the nose two lovers hide, as though separated by a mountain. To meet, to touch, they must go down together into the cavity that opens up in the heart. That is their bedroom. There they twine in coitus. Seen from outside, the eyes of the sleepers are hidden by the eyelids as though by a curtain around a bed. Meanwhile, in the heart's cavity, Indra and Indrani are one inside the other. This is the supreme beatitude.

What is truly extraordinary, as Calasso convincingly shows in *Literature and the Gods*, is that in the guise of what he calls "absolute literature" some of the mythic Indian ideas seem to reappear in the West. He is not talking about direct influence of Indian thought or mythology, which was largely unknown in the nineteenth century, but of an authentic independent discovery by Western poets of similar perceptions. Of course, before any of that was possible, poetry had to free itself from the obligation to be socially relevant. Poets were now saying that poetry is like music, a language that cannot be paraphrased into another language. It is a knowledge that refuses to be subject to any other knowledge, in touch with the nameless origins of everything, the home of even the gods themselves.

•

One gets a better idea of what Calasso has in mind from his lecture on Isidore Ducasse, the nineteenth-century French poet who wrote under the name of the Comte de Lautréamont. *Les Chants de Maldoror*, that notorious work of macabre humor and hallucinatory erotic imagery, was written, as he says, "on the principle that *anything* and *everything* must be the object of sarcasm," not just the posturings of his contemporaries with their sniveling self-pity and Romantic melancholy, but even those who raged against it like Baudelaire. Before he died at the age of twenty-four in 1870, Ducasse lived entirely in books. He drew all his material from them, freely stole passages from classics and rewrote them reversing their meanings. *Chants* in the title makes one expect a book of songs, perhaps a French equivalent of *Song of Myself*. Instead, we find an anti-Whitman who exults in mixing up genres. As his translator Alexis Lykiard noted, in Ducasse we get prose poetry, poetic prose, the Gothic fantasy, the serial novel, horror and humor, authorial interventions, disruptions of space and time, stories within stories, plagiarism, techniques of collage, changes of style as frequent as his hero Maldoror's own metamorphoses, and an elliptical rather than linear structure.

Rimbaud is undoubtedly a better poet, and his *Illuminations* and *A Season in Hell* have been far more influential works, but they lack Ducasse's poisonous air of mockery. For him, writers are stooges and so is every literary propriety. He thought, Calasso writes, that "literature is a continuum of words to be interfered with as one pleases, by transforming every sign into its opposite, if that's what we want." Previously, even the most rebellious literature stayed in touch with some version of the real world. Ducasse got rid of all that. "Any literature that challenges the eternal truths is condemned to feed only on itself," he wrote. And he did just that.

The two finest essays in Calasso's new book are on Stephane Mallarmé. In the century of exact sciences, confident positivism in philosophy, and naturalism and realism in literature, Mallarmé cultivates obscure inner states and speaks approvingly of an art consecrated to fictions. In a piece based on a lecture given at Oxford and Cambridge universities in 1894, he writes:

> Description conceals the fullness and intrinsic virtues of monuments, the sea and the human face; evocation, *allusion* or *suggestion*, though somewhat casual terms, point to what may be a very decisive trend in literature, one which both limits and sets free; for the special charm of the art lies not in the handful of dust, so to speak, not in the containing of any reality through description, in a book or a text, but in freeing from it the spirit, that volatile dispersion which is the musicality of nothing.[3]

Here modern literature and ancient myths meet. Without knowing the Vedic texts and with only a superficial acquaintance with Buddhism, Mallarmé was trying to give a name to a process at the heart of old esoteric traditions. It kept eluding him, but he made great poetry out of his inability to do so. "There must be something occult in the ground of everyone" is how he described it in a letter. "I firmly believe in something hidden away, a closed and secret signifier, that

---

3. *Symbolism: An Anthology*, ed. and trans. by T. G. West (London: Methuen, 1980), 8.

inhabits the ordinary." "Yes, I *know*," he writes in another letter, "we are nothing but vain forms of matter—yet sublime too when you think that we invented God and our own souls." About Mallarmé Calasso writes that never had poetry been so magnificently superimposed upon the most mysterious and elementary fact of all, the very medium in which every quality and every likeness appear, and which is called consciousness. What draws him to Mallarmé is the poet's recognition of that truth, which Calasso himself has chased after in all his books. For them, as for Heidegger, thinking of Being is the only way to deal with poetry.[4] In their different ways they also have a longing for the absolute and are ready to go for broke. For them, the game of being and nothingness is the supreme game, the only one worth playing.

•

"There is a very strong and very ancient emotion," Calasso writes, "that is rarely mentioned or recognized: it is the anguish we feel for the absence of idols. If the eye has no image on which to rest, if there's nothing to mediate between the mental phantasm and that which simply is, then a subtle despondency creeps in." The oldest dream ever recorded, it turns out, is told by a woman, the overseer of a palace in Mesopotamia, who in her dream enters the temple and finds that the statues have vanished and so have the people who worshiped them. For Calasso, literature is the guardian of every such space haunted by phantoms. "For whatever they may be, the gods manifest themselves above all as mental events. Yet, contrary to the modern illusion, it is the psychic powers that are fragments of the gods, not the gods that are fragments of the psychic powers." Before they could come back, literature had to find again that place, inscribed in the very ground of our being, where they have always made their presence known.

---

4. For Calasso's reflections on Heidegger, Kafka, Flaubert, Nietzsche, Marx, Freud, Walter Benjamin, and Karl Kraus, among others, see the collection of his essays, *Forty-Nine Steps*, translated by John Shepley, published by the University of Minnesota Press.

Mallarmé has been both an ideal and a dead end for poets. His greatness, Octavio Paz, wrote, "lies not just in his attempt to create a language that would be the magic double of the universe—the Work conceived as a Cosmos—but above all in the consciousness of the impossibility of transforming that language into theater, into a dialogue with man."[5] Once there's nothing left but a few cryptic words for the initiates, what started out as a new understanding of aesthetics has turned into mysticism. A poem cannot be pure: it is a marriage of contradictions, reverence and blasphemy, asceticism and sensuality. As much as I admire Calasso's uncompromising search for the heart of the poetic, I'm not convinced that such a search is the best way to go about writing poetry. The most attractive and puzzling aspect of the long history of poetry is that no conception of the poem is final.

Literature is never the product of a single agent, Calasso tells us. There are always at least three actors: the hand that writes, the voice that speaks, the god who watches over and compels. They could be called the I, the Self, and the Divine. The relationship between them is constantly changing as they take turns viewing themselves and the world. Mallarmé, he says, gave notice that having left by society's front door, literature was back through a cosmic window, having absorbed in the meantime nothing less than everything. Calasso concludes his study by saying that we still draw sustenance from this "daring fiction." We undoubtedly do, while reminding ourselves that the search for the absolute doesn't always take place in such a rarefied atmosphere, but has to contend with everything else human beings do, from tossing and turning all night with a toothache to falling in love with someone who doesn't care whether you exist. The best critique of absolute literature is to be found in Calasso's two books on myth where that crowning paradox is never forgotten. Besides, as he himself has told us, the gods get bored with men who have no stories to tell.

---

5. *The Bow and the Lyre*, translated by Ruth L. C. Simms (Austin: University of Texas Press, 1973), 44–45.

JOHN BANVILLE

THE IDOLATRY OF LIGHT[1]

Giambattista Tiepolo was not the last of the old masters—that dubious distinction is usually conferred on Goya—but it is surely safe to say that he was the last great painter of the Italian Renaissance. In Roberto Calasso's elegant formulation, Tiepolo was "the right person to impersonate painting's epilogue, just as in a theater performance there is an actor whose function is solely to appear at the end and make an imperfectible bow to the audience." Although Tiepolo was born on the cusp of the seventeenth century, his work strongly echoes that of earlier painters, especially Veronese, who died more than a century before Tiepolo's birth but whose themes, subjects, and even turns of style Tiepolo freely borrowed from. Calasso quotes a contemporary's estimation of Tiepolo as "a happy painter by nature," and Calasso himself goes so far as to describe him as "the last breath of happiness in Europe." It is all more complicated than that, of course; and it is the complexities here, as so often elsewhere, that Calasso finds most stimulating.

Very little is known of Tiepolo the man. His family bore an anciently aristocratic name, but this was either a happy coincidence or a deliberate borrowing. As Michael Levey says in his fine and detailed monograph on the painter, which first appeared in 1986, Tiepolo does not seem to have claimed kinship with the noble Venetian family, "but it is likely that somehow a member of it had adopted an ancestor of the painter's and permitted, or encouraged, use of the name." We do know that he was born on April 16, 1696, to Domenico and Orsetta Tiepolo, the youngest of their six children. On the baptismal entry the painter's father is listed merely as "merchant," but in the Venice of the day that

1. Originally published in *The New Republic* on June 5, 2010. Reprinted with permission of the author.

could have meant anything from a lowly dealer in olive oil to a mighty magnate with a flotilla of ships at his command. Certainly Domenico had contacts among the leading Venetian families, for instance the Dolfin, who were to commission some of the painter's early works.

Was Tiepolo secretive, an artistic cabbalist who hid his doings from the world, or was he just careless of history's hunger for biographical facts? Certainly, as Calasso writes, "his life was as transparent as glass: no one noticed it." His few personal appearances in his work are tinged with sly humor, as in the surely intentional comedy of *Apelles Painting Campaspe*, where everyone, not least the painter, seems amazed at what is going on, or in *Rachel Hiding the Idols from Her Father Laban*, from which a decidedly unflattering self-portrait looks out at us with an ironical cast, as if, Levey writes, "inviting a smile at the extravagant spectacle of which he is the deviser." (And at the painter's feet, delightfully, sits a little girl who is a dead ringer for Maggie Simpson.) He was recognized from early on as supremely gifted, "with an imagination daring and ardent," as Levey nicely has it, and around 1710 he entered the Venetian studio of Gregorio Lazzarini to be trained as a painter. Apart from the all-pervading influence of Veronese, Tiepolo also absorbed the lessons of past masters such as Rembrandt and Salvator Rosa, and the example of his older contemporary Giambattista Piazzetta. Tiepolo and Piazzetta differed in many respects— Levey describes them as the Picasso and Matisse of their time—but the effect of the older painter's work on that of the younger is plain. Levey writes:

> What Tiepolo was responding to was the forceful yet not coarse or exaggerated realism that Piazzetta conveyed, as much in his accomplished, admired drawings [. . .] as in his paintings. Physical actuality, summed up in the body, was grasped with an originality that embraced idiosyncratic types of physiognomy, consciously ordinary, even plebeian, but exuding a challenging, pungent air of being "true."

•

Roberto Calasso acknowledges the "physical actuality" of Tiepolo's work, but what he chooses to emphasize is precisely the painter's lack of emphasis. For Calasso, what marks Tiepolo off from the other great Italian painters, even Veronese, is the way in which he gives himself up to that phenomenon which, Calasso suggests, is the "ultimate peculiarity of Italian culture, the quality it could be proudest of," that is, *sprezzatura*. This slippery word—hardly translatable, so deeply is it woven into the language and life of Italy—is defined by Castiglione, so Calasso tells us, as the avoidance of affectation by "using in all things a certain nonchalance [*sprezzatura*] that may conceal art and demonstrate that what one does and says is done without effort and almost without thinking." The perils of characterizing an artist's work in this way are obvious—nonchalance can seem mere whimsy, and betray a fatal dandyism—and much of Calasso's book is devoted to demonstrating that it is precisely in the lightness of his touch that Tiepolo achieves his weightiest effects.

A hundred years ago, the painter John Butler Yeats, writing from self-imposed exile in New York, gave a wise piece of advice to his son William: an artist, the old man cautioned, must have a great facility—*and never use it*. Tiepolo's facility, particularly as a fresco artist, was legendary: has there ever been a painter who solved with such elegance and such seeming ease the problem of situating figures in space? This extraordinary talent has led a number of commentators, who should have known better, to dismiss him as a mere provider of overblown triumphs and trumperies to the wealthy aristocrats who hired him to adorn their grand dwellings and puff up their already high regard for themselves.

It is true that Tiepolo worked hard, at extraordinary speed, to satisfy the desires of his patrons, from Dionisio Dolfin, for whom he painted some of his earliest works at the patriarchal palace at Udine, through Karl Philipp von Greiffenklau, Prince-Bishop of Würzburg, the ceilings of whose Neue Residenz he decorated with what are considered his greatest frescoes, to

Charles III of Spain, who summoned him to paint the throne room of the Royal Palace of Madrid, the city where Tiepolo died in 1770. All this hectic busyness struck suspicion into many a stout heart of the late-Romantic age. "There were years," Calasso remarks, "in which English-speaking travelers visited Venice and did not see Tiepolo." Ruskin disdained his work, and Henry James tells us of writing in "one of the faded back rooms" of the Palazzo Barbaro in Venice under a "pompous Tiepolo ceiling."

On the other hand, and somewhat surprisingly, Mark Twain in 1878 wrote in his diary: "But Tiepolo is *my* artist," and James's friend Edith Wharton, Calasso tellingly observes, "admired Tiepolo without moral reservations, with upper-class confidence." We might have expected Proust to revel in the work of this great Venetian, but in all of *In Search of Lost Time*, Calasso assures us—trust him to know a thing like this—there is no mention of any Tiepolo painting, though the name occurs three times, each time in the context of a shade of red. "Perhaps," Calasso writes, "the most congenial and equable end for an artist is that of being transformed into a color, like Daphne into laurel: this is what happened to Tiepolo in Proust," who on various occasions dresses the three most significant women in his work—Odette, the Duchesse de Guermantes, and Albertine—in "Tiepolo pink."

Calasso's remark about Edith Wharton's "upper-class confidence" is a sort of limbering-up preparatory to his defensive assault on the great Italian critic Roberto Longhi, who "made Tiepolo the Bad Guy to set in opposition to the Good Guy par excellence, who was unfailingly Caravaggio." Longhi, unusually for such a patrician and finical discriminator, wrote a rancorous fictional dialogue between Caravaggio and Tiepolo supposed to take place in heaven—"a whimsy without precedent or further development in Longhi's work"—in which Caravaggio berates his younger colleague for not being sufficiently dedicated to "truth." Calasso describes Longhi's "rant" against Tiepolo as "not entirely unlike an altercation between neighbors in a condo, albeit one conducted in a high-flown style," a description which could be applied equally well to Calasso's own shouting match with his late fellow critic.

•

Ruskin, in his dismissal of Tiepolo, spoke of him as "virtually the beginner of Modernism" and went on to compare paintings of his to "what a first-rate Parisian Academy student would do . . . after having read unlimited quantities of George Sand and Dumas." It is profoundly ironic, Calasso observes, that

> the word *modernism*, which throughout the twentieth century would become the emblem of all avant-garde movements, is here applied to the most hackneyed academic painting, which in its turn could allegedly be traced back to Tiepolo. Yet now that the clamor of the avant-garde has passed, saying that Tiepolo had something to do with modernism makes sense once more.

Calasso in his book has two broad aims. The first is to convince us of Tiepolo's position as the last great practitioner of European painting, "at least in the particular, singular, irretrievable sense it had acquired over roughly five centuries in Europe, where countless painters had all conformed to a single notion of painting and moved as a unified whole of immaculate grace and lightness, like certain extremely fat actors such as Sydney Greenstreet." (Calasso has an endearing tendency to lurch into the vernacular.) The second, and related, aim is to defend Tiepolo against the "partisan poetics" of vaguely left-wing critics such as Longhi, whose dedication to "the ideology of *realismo all'italiana*" as represented by Caravaggio blinded him, Calasso believes, to Tiepolo's true worth.

Thus Calasso observes that "while it is doubtful that the cause of the proletariat was dear to his heart," Longhi out of political conviction insisted on the term *reality* as an arbiter of artistic success, "and always with the idea that modernism must be, by vocation, something grim and 'workaday'"— rather than, we assume, airy and easeful, and ever informed by the spirit of *sprezzatura*. Calasso sees himself agreeing with Longhi that Tiepolo was the last of a glorious line, but for Longhi Tiepolo was "the weak link [. . .] the reprobate whose aberrant style heralded the lamentable end of a superb history." While Longhi claimed Caravaggio as the first painter of the modern age, Calasso on the contrary insists that "in retrospect the only painter who could have had a claim to be the first of the forefathers of 'modern life' was none other than Tiepolo."

The spectacle of one scholar lambasting another is always fun for the rest of us, but the intricate argument that Calasso engages in here is an important one. It broaches nothing less than the sources and the purposes of art itself. Tiepolo's *realismo* is of a separate order—"Tiepolo's characters form a parallel world, with its own customs and conventions"—and his truth is not the truth of brute facts. Far more than the self-willed Caravaggio, Tiepolo is for Calasso a true leveler, leading his tribe of characters, "the prophetic tribe with blazing eyes" that Baudelaire speaks of in *Les Fleurs du Mal*, from Venice to Würzburg to Madrid and back again, "an unstoppable motley caravan that dragged along with them all their assorted trappings, the flotsam and jetsam of history." Calasso sees in this troupe of commedia dell'arte players—surprisingly, there is no mention of Watteau, another artist whose essence is evanescence—an invention "one might dream about to this day: a democracy leveled off toward the top, where aesthetic quality makes it possible to eliminate any divergence in status."

And then there is the sheer happiness that Tiepolo communicates—that happiness for which "he was not forgiven." It is a rapturous conjuring of delight out of light: Calasso quotes Giorgio Manganelli speaking of Tiepolo as "an idolater of light disguised as a human being," and himself defines him as "the saturnine painter of radiant light." Longhi, too, "when he was not blinded by acrimony," had a wonderful notion of Tiepolo as "a Veronese after a downpour," and indeed these depthless skyscapes have the thrilling instability of rain-light. In Tiepolo, it is always a rinsed and glistening April afternoon. And in that luminous, languorous *après-midi* it is Eros that rules: "Every fiber of his painting is erotic. Not only in the bodies and poses but in the *ductus*, which washes over his figures like a wave of light." No wonder the princes and the worldly churchmen loved him.

•

The central section of Calasso's book is a detailed study of thirty-three remarkable and mysterious etchings by Tiepolo, ten *Capricci* and twenty-three *Scherzi*, the dating of which is disputed, though it seems the *Capricci* were made in the 1740s and the *Scherzi* in the 1750s. "There is a sense," Michael Levey wrote, "in which the *Scherzi di Fantasia* could be claimed as the most perfect productions of all Tiepolo's art." These strange, obsessively repetitive works have puzzled most scholars and made many of them palpably uneasy, not only because of their enigmatic quality but also because of the dark matters in which they dabble: satyr families, mysterious Orientals, severed heads, baleful owls, and ubiquitous serpents, usually twined around staves, as with the caduceus of Hermes. The book's well-written blurb is a little misleading in promising us that, while few have attempted to tackle the mystery of these etchings, "Roberto Calasso rises to the challenge, interpreting them as chapters in a dark narrative that contains the secrets of Tiepolo's art." Tackle them he does, and with great verve; but when it comes to his actual interpretation of these obscure poetic images, there is a great deal of throat-clearing and shuffling of papers, as the scholar takes refuge behind his scholarship.

Certainly Calasso writes wonderfully about the series—for instance, when he describes how they are "marked by the convergence of a superabundance of light and a kind of internal corrosion of the objects," and how in them "Tiepolo wove the countermelody of the Enlightenment." But as to the essential riddle of these sphinxlike works, he is more modest than his blurb writer. It is unclear, he writes, why the airiest of painters, the one most accustomed to moving among skies and clouds, should have cultivated and developed—in the secret chamber of his mind—this chain of images of claustrophobia *en plein air*, charged with burning intensity. Images that all—even the scholars most faithful to Tiepolo, like Levey—seem to wish to flee from as fast as possible, murmuring a few words of cursory admiration. If the *Scherzi* are Tiepolo's secret, then it must also be admitted that it is a well-protected one.

As to scholarship, Calasso ranges from hermeneutic probings of the Book of Genesis through the Eleusinian Mysteries and the works of Hermes Trismegistus to the Rig-Veda and the sermons of Saint Ambrose. This writer is nothing if not well-read—a fact which he is eager to impress upon us and about which he is perhaps a little vain. His interrogation of these works is marvelously stimulating, but he, too, ends in vagueness and vague unease. A "suspicion begins slowly to creep in," he tells us "that the subject of the *Scherzi* is seeing—and observing oneself." The word "scherzo" in one of its meanings signifies a joke, and perhaps the "'joke' that the *Scherzi* conceal in their gravity would be this: they are images that look at themselves." That may be—but really, what does it signify?

In the end, however, it does not matter. Explorers cannot be blamed if sometimes their sites keep their secrets. And we do not go to a book such as this one in expectation of an Agatha Christie plot neatly unpicked. Calasso has written a brilliant, eccentric, provocative, annoying, and thoroughly splendid celebration of a great painter the essence of whose work, as with the work of all real artists, must remain enigmatic:

> Nowhere was he recognized for what he was, nor did anyone grasp the peculiarity of the spell cast by his hand. Just as he had arrived without meeting any resistance, so he departed without arousing any

regret, losing himself among the names of those of whom there is a confused, shadowy memory. No one suspected that with him vanished the last point of equilibrium in the visible. Elusive, precarious, and bewitching. Yet such was the case. Thereafter, even the possibility that that point existed was forgotten.

ANDREA LEE

ROBERTO CALASSO'S ENCYCLOPEDIC MIND AT PLAY[1]

Recently, I read Roberto Calasso's *La Folie Baudelaire*, which brought back to mind a half hour that I spent, years ago, wandering with the author through the Milan train station, looking for *Mad* magazine. After an interview for a *New Yorker* profile I was writing about him, he'd politely accompanied me to the Turin train and then stayed to share my perambulation from foreign-language newsstand to newsstand in search of the magazine I had promised my daughter. It was a rainy afternoon: we drank coffee at a bleak linoleum bar that no longer exists and then strolled around in the gloomy station with its huge dripping vault and its allegorical statues streaked with pigeon droppings, enjoying the sight of the hurrying crowd and the puffing engines, and swapping sophomoric quips about the deep meaning of "Spy vs. Spy." I remember being unsurprised that the terrifyingly erudite Calasso, who resembled a slightly glum faun in a trench coat and whose hair curled around the edges of his balding head like a permanent wreath of laurels, knew and liked *Mad*.

I also recall feeling that this dark, meandering quest for something goofy yet possibly profound was an elemental Calasso experience: in every way corresponding to the style in which he lives with an astonishing coherence possible for few literary figures today. As one of the preeminent authors in Italy, he has, in a country that, in spirit, has never ceased to be a collection of small principalities, created his own small but powerful Republic of Letters as head of the legendary Milanese publishing house Adelphi. Here, for over thirty years he has produced a remarkable eclectic line of books, whose elegant black spines and muted colors fill entire walls in the houses of Italians with

---

1. Originally published by *The New Yorker*, December 13, 2012. Copyright © 2012 by Andrea Lee. Reprinted with permission of the author.

any claim to high culture. Adelphi authors range from Simenon to Athanasius Kircher to Anna Maria Ortese—a collection almost exclusively shaped by the personal appeal of each to the subtle fancy of Calasso, who lives for books and ideas in a way that goes beyond the hermetic existence of the most unworldly university professor and seems to take him outside of time and space. In conferences, he sometimes describes the tradition of literature as a kind of living creature, a "serpent of books" winding its way through the centuries, that is clearly vivid in his imagination. Some vertebrae of the serpent are composed of Calasso's own magnum opus, an encyclopedic series of linked volumes that he began with *The Ruin of Kasch*, in 1989, and explore the relation of myth to the birth of modern consciousness.

Calasso has created a much discussed original genre for these books, which are neither fiction or nonfiction but a dense pastiche of myth, biography, criticism, philosophy, history, and minutiae, studded with quotations and woven together by Calasso's unflagging vision until they take on a kind of organic life of their own. Rather than exploring ideas, his books invoke spirits—of places, cultural periods, personalities. Although they seem to deal with wildly heterogeneous subjects, each book is linked to the others by its ample, universalist style—with a Cecil B. DeMille-size cast of artists, thinkers, hangers-on ,and divinities large and small—and recurrent themes. The assembled volumes form a distinct constellation in Calasso's interior universe.

In *Kasch*, Calasso links an African Tower of Babel legend with the life of "the first modern man," Talleyrand—with stops on the way at Freud, Marx, and every other possible influential modern thinker. From there, Calasso passes to a sweeping evocation of the spirit of Greek mythology (*The Marriage of Cadmus and Harmony*, 1988); to a still more sweeping retelling of the *Mahābhārata* (*Ka*, 1996); to a meditation on the world of Kafka (*K.*, 2002); to an examination of the divine sprezzatura and esoteric underside of prerevolutionary eighteenth-century Europe (*Tiepolo Pink*, 2006); and so to the dark nineteenth century of *La Folie Baudelaire*, which Farrar, Straus and Giroux has just published in Alastair McEwen's lively English translation. (The seventh book in the series, *L'Ardore*, not yet translated into English, returns to the subject of India in a five-hundred-page discussion of the Vedas.) Together, the series presents Calasso's panoramic vision of human creativity as a cyclical force constantly in motion—sometimes in a violent fall from innocence—away from its collective roots in myth and ritual toward extremes of originality in the hands of great artists, from whence it inevitably begins a return towards its origins.

La Folie Baudelaire examines the father of Symbolist poetry as founder and symptom of the contagion that would be soon defined as "the modern." Baudelaire in this role has made already brief appearances in Calasso's books. Early in *Kasch*, the author writes: "At a time when the German romantics are still talking about ideas, Baudelaire blends theological asides with the smells of the streets, the nausea of manifestos, urban happenstance, itemizations of debts and recipes using Icelandic lichens. It's as if a side curtain were shockingly pulled aside to reveal the person while onstage the same old performance continues."

Five books later, the poet is in a starring role, as Calasso uses his life and work, particularly his extraordinary art criticism, as a lens to contemplate the explosive cultural transformation of the early modern period. Calasso's book can be seen as a series of spirited improvisations on the theme expressed in Walter Benjamin's essays on Baudelaire: that the poet, though he remained resolutely in the Romantic tradition, was the first to express the dark new reality of what Benjamin called "the permanent catastrophe" of life after the Industrial Revolution. Calasso illuminates this image of Baudelaire: the first poet to describe the shocking beauty of a decomposing corpse; to define the mixture of disgust, boredom, alienation, and fear that hung like a permanent fever mist in the brain of the city-dweller; to glory in the allure of the unhealthy, perverse and deformed, of the artificial and mechanical, of dissonance and fragmentation—all the scenery of destruction and despair that would become the natural landscape of writers from Kafka to Sartre and onward.

Half of the book is devoted to characters personally or spiritually connected to Baudelaire: friends, enemies, lovers, artistic heirs, tenuous acquaintances, admirers, writers, and painters he detested or admired: a cast ranging from such figures as Ingres, Delacroix, and Rimbaud to minor but essential characters like the luminous artists' muse, Madame Sabatier, and the elusive Constantin Guys, the illustrator who captured the equivocal spirit of contemporary Parisian life. The pages of *Baudelaire* swarm with their loves, feuds, manias, and the minutiae of their daily lives, and illustrate the way their idiosyncratic visions cross-fertilized to give the period its peculiar flavor.

Calasso gives order to this sea of names and details by framing his text with three powerful images of Baudelaire. The book opens with the first: a subtly disturbing note written by the poet to his mother Caroline, inviting her, in the insinuating tone of a clandestine lover, to meet him at the Louvre. Calasso's stage is set, his hero announced, in just these few words, with their suggestion of perversity clothed in propriety; their strange hint that a museum could be confounded with a house of assignation; the uncomfortable contrast they set up between public and private; the general darkness that lies just their surface.

The second image, at the center of the book, also involves a museum: it is Baudelaire's famous dream, in which he explores a vast and labyrinthine exhibition hall that is simultaneously a whorehouse, filled with a mixture of great art and seedy pornography. The place has a numinous feel, like the cave in the primal dream that Jung describes in *Memories, Dreams, Reflections*; but at the center, instead of the enthroned phallus that Jung sees, the poet meets his own soul in the form of a living work of art: a human chimera deformed by a monstrous cranial growth resembling both an umbilical cord and a twining serpent. Calasso adds impact to this dramatic encounter by pointing out that the monster resembles Phanes, the serpent-bound god of the Eleusinian Mysteries—a figure who happens also to pop up in Calasso's *Cadmus and Harmony* as "firstborn of the world of appearances, the key to the mind."

The third image, from which *La Folie Baudelaire* draws its title, was coined by Baudelaire's nemesis, the viciously brilliant Saint-Beuve. The famous critic described the poet's work as a *folie*, or architectural folly—a fanciful, Romantic-era pavilion—a folly not, however, surrounded by the comfortable landscapes of Europe but built beyond the reach of civilization on the icy wasteland of the Kamchatka Peninsula. Calasso is at his best as he playfully expands the metaphor, suggesting that, rather than being an anchorite, Baudelaire was actually a pioneer, whose fanciful construction eventually formed the nucleus of a settlement of his cultural heirs, from Rimbaud and Laforgue to Proust, Nietszche, Chopin, Kafka, and Wagner. It is a perfect conceit: the Modernist period as a mad artists' colony, a sort of Provincetown of teetering, eccentric cottages constructed from debris of the past, each defiantly different from the other, but connected by a common debt to the first settler.

To imagine oneself exploring the mazy paths of a village of eccentric geniuses—or drifting, Walter Benjamin style, through a crowded Parisian arcade—is a useful device for any reader of *Baudelaire* and the rest of Calasso's sometimes daunting oeuvre. Calasso could be speaking of himself when, discussing Baudelaire's art criticism, he observes that Baudelaire "had no talent for any form of linear development." If an unwary reader plunges into the undergrowth of names and citations expecting to tramp down an expository trail, he risks collapse from a sort of private Stendhal syndrome—or perhaps a slow death from exhaustion in the intricate defiles of Calasso's metaphysical excursions.

No, positively the most agreeable way to read these books is to become a literary flâneur, to adopt a meandering pace and a open-minded, mildly impulsive attitude, as if one were lazily following a chain of associations through the Internet. (In fact in this overstimulated age of viral memes, music sampling, and mass ADD, Calasso's agglomerate style seems ever more contemporary.) One learns to ramble through his labyrinthine series of *Wunderkammer*, speeding past what looks unreasonably opaque, pausing here and there to enjoy some mesmerizing bit of trivia. (Who but Calasso, for example, would have unearthed a schoolboyish note written from Baudelaire to Sainte-Beuve about gingerbread?)

Smoothing the way is the curiously conversational tone in which even the most arcane information is conveyed, as well as the underlying sense that, as the author piles detail upon detail, he's having a huge amount of fun. Calasso may identify with his hero, but there is no Baudelairean melancholy in his work. There's no show-off either—only a sincere delight, an innocent reveling in his own encyclopedic mind at play. This mood is catching, and if one adopts the right dreamy pace, one can commune with Calasso through a kind of imaginative osmosis—a word and image the author adores. "Writing," he remarks in *Baudelaire*, "like eros, is what makes the bulkheads of the ego sway and become porous."

After arriving at the outer limits of Kamchatka, *Baudelaire* ends with a hint at the Modernist return to the primal roots of art: a scene in which the poet reflects that an African sculpture, "might be the one true God." In the same way, following *Baudelaire*, Calasso returns to ancient origins to complete his seven-book series. *L'Ardore*, the final volume, takes Vedic sacrifice as its theme, as it explores the birth of form, particularly language, out of chaos as the process appears through the mythological glass of the most venerable of Indian sacred texts. The book—dense with citation even by Calasso standards—has not yet appeared in English, but translating a few lines will serve as further comment on *Baudelaire* and all the rest of Calasso's impossible, enchanting books, which beneath all their fiendish complexity are simple and valiant professions of love for literature—the whole prodigious sum of it, that enormous serpent of books that he envisions twining through history. *L'immanifesto è molto più vasto del manifesto. L'invisible del visibile. Così, anche per il linguaggio . . . Soltanto perché la lingua proietta un ombra ben più vasta di se è inacessibile la parola conserva e rinova un tale incanto.* ("That which is not manifest is much more vast than that which is manifest. The invisible is greater than the visible. So it is also for language . . . Only because language casts a shadow both much vaster than itself, and inaccessible, does the spoken word hold and renew such magic.")

The last time I visited Calasso at his Adelphi office, I brought him a gift: a worn copy of *The Panorama Of Modern Literature*, a 1935 anthology of short works from an extraordinary list of authors then alive: Aldous Huxley, Joseph Conrad, E. B. White, Dorothy Parker, and Stephan Zweig, to name just a few. Calasso looked over the table of contents with the air of a gourmet studying a three-star menu, then gave one of his rare smiles. "Look at these names! Imagine what a time that was to publish books," he said, looking for a minute perfectly happy to have so many writers in his hands.

FRANCISCO RICO

ON ROBERTO CALASSO'S
CENTO LETTERE A UNO SCONOSCIUTO

Evidently, Jorge Luis Borges did not fail to anticipate any possibility: the book that is "the figure and the perfect compendium of all the others"; the book that does not need to be read because it is all in the title; the nonexistent book that is created when it is criticized in a review . . . Roberto Calasso has admitted all of Borges's eventualities, adding one: on the corresponding jacket flaps, he has rewritten one by one the more than thousand books that he has published under the elegant Milanese marque of Adelphi.

A selection of these jacket flaps, illustrating forty years in the life of a singular publishing house and of Calasso's own intellectual project, has been printed under the heading *Cento lettere a uno sconosciuto* [One hundred letters to a stranger]. One might ask whether, as a publisher, this might not backfire. Once they have been read, the majority of books cease to live, except as a residue, or a vague outline in the memory. Why read them, then, if what we retain of most has less substance than a jacket flap? In fact, the penetration, density, and suggestive power of Calasso's flaps transform a hundred Adelphi volumes into a pure and simple documentary appendix to his *Cento lettere*.

The work of Calasso the writer has been widely disseminated in every language, with the result that many readers have been able to enjoy the fluid storytelling that recreates classical mythology in *The Marriage of Cadmus and Harmony*; the radiant rehearsal of the Hindu cosmogony of being, the spirit (*manas*), and the word, in *Ka*; a Kafka from inside Kafka, in *K.*; and the golden age of French literature in *La Folie Baudelaire*.

The Adelphi catalogue is, naturally, less well known outside of Italy. From the beginning, the publishing house welcomed names of great prestige, put other names back into circulation, which were indisputable but rather neglected, and rescued not a few others from oblivion. Nor does Calasso doesn't lack a keen eye, capable of recognizing talented authors just published in any language, to the point that more than one international career has begun with his blessing. But Adelphi's tract is chiefly given over to unexpected rediscoveries and exotic delicacies. It is enough to point out the first and the last of the titles presented in the *Hundred Letters*: *Erewhon*, the caustic upside-down world (Nowhere) of Samuel Butler, and the *Edicts of Ashoka*, conqueror of lands and souls for Buddhism.

Calasso says that in the beginning, in the '60s, not everyone was able to grasp what bound the catalogue together: what was the link between "a fantastical novel, a Japanese treatise on theatrical art, a popular book of ethology, a Tibetan religious text, the story of an imprisonment during the Second World War"? Soon, what bound it together began to be distinguished, with approval and perplexity, precisely in the multiplicity of suggestions and the opening of horizons it implied, in a period when politics hung heavy on the air, and the most visible Italian literature was still neorealism.

This is the *pars destruens*. But if we ask ourselves about the affirmative side and, following Borges, seek out a plausible "figure and compendium" of all of Calasso and Adelphi's books, we must go back to the motto exhibited on the jacket flap of Manganelli's *La letteratura come menzogna* (1985), which is later developed in *Literature and the Gods*, and will perhaps accompany Calasso for the rest of his life: "absolute literature."

The premise of "absolute literature" is that truth can be arrived at only through the falsity of a complete invention. Thence, since romanticism, the gods have returned to literature as a place of unparalleled experience—the only one that, setting up camp outside society, at the edge of the sordid Leviathan, consents to come into contact with a truth of another order, which is deeper, mysterious, ultimately divine. "Absolute literature" is experienced through "a certain vibration or luminosity" that "makes visible what otherwise would be impossible to see" and lets us discover the world as myth.

The theory can be discussed all you like, but in the end few will be unwilling to admit that good literature casts reality in a different light (from another perspective, a marvelous book by Mario Vargas Llosa, for example, has insisted on "the truth of lies") and, anyway, it is impossible not to appreciate the sumptuous fruits that Calasso has produced as a writer and as a publisher. Attempts to replicate the Adelphi catalog in other countries have been useless, however. The success of the Milanese publishing house is difficult to export, as it largely answers to an Italian cultural particularity.

With rare divagations, Italian literature has always proceeded along a path separate from the real, rejecting any "open compromise with historical and social reality" (Carlo Dionisotti), and seeking instead what is atemporally sublime, distant from the language and the landscape of everyday life. For material and background, *The Marriage of Cadmus and Harmony* and *Literature and the Gods* both pick up the thread of Boccaccio's *Genealogiae deorum gentilium*, with their exaltation of poetry as a knowledge of truth usually thought to belong to philosophy and theology. "Absolute literature" is at bottom the idea that Bembo, the supreme dictator, indisputably imposes: writing "*divina atque absolutissima.*" While in Italy, Calasso and Adelphi are frequently accused of being inauthentic, a province of the imaginary empire of Mitteleuropa, from the other side of the Alps, they appear to us in radical agreement with the most illustrious Italian tradition. Governed, of course, as an absolute monarchy.

This aristocratic character—of "high" (as it's written in Italian) rank—in Italian letters has also been to the benefit of our Milanese friends in other respects. Adelphi's books are impeccable in their paper, their printing, and their typography. This is no less true in matters of content, which are sadly neglected at other houses. I suspect that Calasso would be willing to chop off his own finger rather than to allow a Sanskrit term or the name of Leoš Janáček to be printed without each of its diacritical marks. But if to go arm in arm with Aldo Manuzio, he has published the phantasmagoric *Hypnerotomachia Poliphili*, he has not limited himself to presenting a facsimile and a translation: he has added prologues and exhaustive notes.

He did not reprint the adventures of Marco Polo in a flimsy "paperback," but in Valeria Bertolucci's critical edition. He has published more Nietzsche than anyone else, but with an extraordinary scholarly apparatus; not to mention that in *Cadmus and Harmony* or in *Ka* the rigor of philology surrenders nothing to the charm of mythology. In these and many other respects, Calasso's exactitude has been just as absolute as his ideal of literature, and the Italian public has accepted this humbly (along with the consequent prices) because they have been prepared for it by centuries of "high" literature. It is often, besides, precisely this extreme exactitude that has led them to value products with the Adelphi label unconditionally.

Calasso's jacket flaps are not summaries, or slogans, or reviews, but absolute pages, with their own scale. They make for pleasant and instructive reading. The fact that some of the titles and authors most representative of Adelphi are missing from the *Cento lettere a uno sconosciuto* implies that the hundred texts chosen do not pretend to provide a compendious image of the catalogue. This Milanese from Florence has not been content to cultivate "publishing" as a literary genre: he wanted and has been able to take possession of all the books he has published by others, and he has fused them with his own writing in a single book. The *Cento lettere* are only one chapter of this inexhaustible volume and of this fathomless ambition.

Translated from the Italian by Alex Andriesse

JORGE HERRALDE

ROBERTO CALASSO, RECIPIENT OF THE PRIX FORMENTOR

In 2003, a very beautiful and voluminous artifact appeared with the title *Adelphiana*, commemorating the fiftieth anniversary of the publishing house Adelphi, preceded by a text by Roberto Calasso, in which he writes: "The challenge has been to go, step by step, through a jungle of more than two thousand titles, letting the air of time filter in." And adds a footnote, with an essential piece of information: "Among all the vices, no one can say stubbornness has been lacking." (Certainly not.)

I am going to speak, as a colleague, about our friendship, and above all about his publishing career and his reflections on our profession in his indispensable little book, *The Art of the Publisher*, a condensation of his great knowledge and his many professional convictions.

We are faced with a quite singular, possibly unique case: a great editor, of long standing, who has at the same time developed a wide-ranging, ambitious, and highly regarded literary oeuvre.

Adelphi was born in 1963 and Anagrama in 1969. We first met in the early '70s and since then have come together over countless dinners and cocktails, at parties or in conversations at our stands, or for brief encounters in the hallways in Frankfurt. And again in Barcelona, where we have had events for so many of his books. And in Turin, Milan, and London, and at the Guadalajara Book Fair. An uninterrupted relationship, both personal and professional, that very often—to use an expression of the great Sergio Pitol's—has been "blessed by laughter."

In "Singular Books," Calasso recounts Adelphi's early years, when it was helmed by Luciano Foà, who after ten years as secretary general at Einaudi decided to do something radically different, following one golden rule: "In a publishing house, as in a book, nothing is irrelevant, nothing is unworthy of full consideration." And Calasso describes Foà: "Physically, he resembled an Egyptian scribe, crouched with his tablet between his legs, gazing fixedly in front of him. Like the scribe, he knew his task was to transmit with maximum precision something memorable, whether a list of provisions or a ritual text. No more, no less. He was interested only in getting to the bottom."

Another who laid the groundwork of Adelphi was Bobi Bazlen, legendary reader, who aspired to a critical edition of Nietzsche and a collection of classics, and also to disseminating a series of books that had not been published by Einaudi and other imprints (among his editorial reports, edited by Calasso, there is a long list of enthusiasms which were not greeted with a positive response). These were what Bazlen called "singular books." Writes Calasso: "The most eloquent example is volume no. 1 in the Biblioteca series: Alfred Kubin's *The Other Side*. It is a singular novel by a non-novelist, in which the reader is drawn into a frightening hallucination. A book written in a state of delirium that lasted three months. [. . .] In short, a singular book is one in which it is clear that *something has happened* to the author and has been put into writing."

Even in the preliminary stages of Adelphi, a very young Calasso was present: "When Bazlen talked to me for the first time about the new publishing house that would become Adelphi—I can give the exact date and place, since it was my twenty-first birthday, in May 1962."

Thus, a long journey begins with the critical edition of Nietzsche and the "singular books." Then, between 1970 and 1980, by means of the Biblioteca Adelphi, the star collection, Calasso writes, "the enduring link [was forged] between Adelphi and Mitteleuropa" (Hofmannsthal, Kraus, Loos, Horváth, Roth, Schnitzler, Canetti, and Wittgenstein, followed by many others). And bookshop wanderers, readers, and critics could now make out what the hell Adelphi was about, and get over "the bewildering lack of connection" among those singular books so different from each other. Suddenly, *tout se tient*, everything is linked: there was "the recognition of a clear connection," Calasso *dixit*.

At this point, a fan unfurls and, in addition to his philosophical and scientific interests, his dedication to the East, India, and Mitteleuropean rescues, extraordinary authors of the best contemporary literature burst into Adelphi, carrying the publishing house to its greater splendor, and to its maximum diffusion among readers. The list is very long: there is the explosion of Kundera, Sebald, Coetzee, Walcott, Faulkner, Naipaul, Chatwin, Szymborska, Burroughs, and, naturally, Nabokov.

Special mention must be made of *i miracoli Calasso*: how to transform Simenon, *dopo il lavoro Adelphi*, a little-regarded writer of kiosk novels into a fundamental literary author (long before Gallimard had accepted him into La Bibliothèque de la Pléiade) and, moreover, one of the house's most infallible long-sellers. More *miracoli*: when the Mitteleuropean vein seemed definitively exhausted, he rescues Sándor Márai from obscurity and rediscovers Irène Némirovsky. Or he starts publishing Carrère, beginning with *Limonov*, to overwhelming success—and also Yasmina Reza, with *Happy Are the Happy*. More difficult still: two Anglo-Saxon writers of modest prominence in their own countries, Cathleen Schine and Patrick McGrath, become bestsellers, but only in Italy. *Auntie Mame* reappears triumphantly. (Some other stunts don't turn out so well; not even magic Adelphi is always infallible: as is logical, Calasso regrets the error . . . naturally the error of readers and critics, who have not been up to the task.)

Despite my tenacious insistence, he does not frequent the Spanish field nearly often enough, but no less than the Libraries of Borges and Bolaño figure in Adelphi's catalogue, where the latter was given a second chance with *2666* and then had all his work recovered. In *The Art of the Publisher*, Calasso comments on the case of Gaston Gallimard, and how one of his greatest skills was to give second chances to important authors rejected by some colleague's misguided reading, as happened with Marcel Proust.

In the field of Italian literature, for example, in 1979, there was Salvatore Satta's great novel *The Day of Judgment*, while in the catalog you can find collected the almost complete works of (citing from memory) Gadda, Savinio,

Sciascia, Flaiano, Manganelli, Arbasino, Anna Maria Ortese, Cristina Campo, and many other essential authors.

•

In "Publishing as a Literary Genre," Calasso emphasizes the fundamental concept of form: "Claude Lévi-Strauss suggested we should regard one of the fundamental activities of mankind—namely the elaboration of myths—as a particular form of bricolage. After all, myths are constructed from readymade elements, many deriving from other myths." And he suggests that the art of publishing be considered as a form of bricolage:

> Try to imagine a publishing house as a single text formed not just by the totality of books that have been published there, but also by all its other constituent elements, such as the front covers, cover flaps, publicity, the quantity of copies printed and sold, or the different editions in which the text has been presented. Imagine a publishing house in this way and you will find yourself immersed in a very peculiar landscape, something that you might regard as a literary work in itself, belonging to a genre all its own. [. . .] The first and last criteria of the art of publishing is *form*: the capacity to give form to a plurality of books as though they were the chapters of a single book. And all this while taking care—a passionate and obsessive care—over the appearance of every volume, over the way in which it is presented. And finally—and this is certainly a point of no small importance—taking care of how that book might be sold to the largest number of readers.

"In a publishing house of the kind I'm describing," he concludes, "an *off-key* book is like an off-key chapter in a novel."

Here are some other peremptory affirmations of Calasso: "Above all, the true publisher is the one who has the arrogance to claim that, in principle, none of his books will fall from the hands of any reader through tedium or an unassailable feeling of extraneousness." And also: "The publisher must enjoy reading the books he publishes." He underscores the necessary complicity between publishers and their readership, which "can be created only on the basis of their repeated experiences of not being disappointed. [. . .] One basic rule: to think that what has not disappointed us will not disappoint others."

·

Calasso highlights a paradox: "One of the notions venerated today in whatever branch of industrial activity is that of the *brand*." But "if a publishing house is not conceived as a form [. . .] it is incapable of triggering that magical element—brand power." He considers that the new and powerful figure of the executive manager cannot "but compromise the special quality of the brand itself" and concludes that "no manager has so far been associated with any memorable event in publishing." And he deals succinctly with the role of literary agents: "the agent's judgment can obviously be more acute than what had, at one time, been the judgment of the publisher. But the agent neither has nor creates a *form*. An agent has only a list of clients." New paragraph. Subject sorted.

And despite dire predictions about publishing, and especially literary publishing, Calasso does not yield: "I wouldn't wish to give the impression that publishing today, in the sense I have attempted to describe—namely publishing where the publisher is happy only if he succeeds in publishing good books—is a lost cause. It is, instead, simply a very tough cause" (date: 2009).

·

In another book, *Literature and the Gods*, he addresses the subject of "absolute literature." That is to say, "'Literature' because it is a knowledge that claims to be accessible only and exclusively by way of literary composition; 'absolute,' because it is a knowledge that one assimilates while in search of an absolute, and that thus draws in no less than everything." According to Calasso, in order to follow "the chequered and tortuous history of absolute literature," we can rely only on writers. And he mentions, among others, Proust, Benn, Valéry, Brodsky, Marina Tsvetaeva, Karl Kraus, Borges, Nabokov, Manganelli, Calvin, Canetti, and Kundera. He also says that everyone is "speaking of the same thing," even though they do not name it. And that this literature can be recognized "by a certain vibration or luminescence of the sentence (or paragraph, or page, or chapter, or whole book even)." "A new shiver" or an "aesthetic shock." To complete this sort of incomplete synthesis of his text, I will quote one of his sentences: "And then along comes Nietzsche and *the* language begins, and all it wants to do, all it can do, is phosphoresce, flash, ravish, amaze."

And, almost to conclude, I will recall my unexpected encounter with *The Ruin of Kasch* (Roberto had kept this project very much a secret) in the mid-eighties, a book that inaugurated, without announcing, Calasso's "work in progress," difficult to define, "helicoidal," as the author points out in an interview, which already runs to eight volumes and which I imagine must have been fundamental for the awarding of this prize. I started reading it on a train on a business trip. And just opening it, I had a bit of a shock: there was something going on.

From the outset, Calasso gives the floor to Talleyrand, who becomes "the book's master of ceremonies, the most clairvoyant and the most detested, the most modern and most archaic of politicians." Among other marks I made while reading the book, one is found, a few pages in, alongside this crackling paragraph:

Indeed, there is a great similarity between Goethe and Talleyrand, those two princely souls! [...] Goethe did not have the impertinence with which Talleyrand held his head, with the semi-closed eye of a charmer, the eye of the languishing viper, since these are spontaneous and natural things that Talleyrand had—gifts of God or of the devil!—whereas nothing is spontaneous and natural in Goethe, this operatic actor, always in front of a mirror . . ."

And so, with this book by Calasso, I had, I imagine, the special shiver that "absolute literature" provokes.

A great and deserved prize, then, for Roberto Calasso—Calasísimo, as we, his friends, call him, with waggish admiration, when he executes one of his unexpected performances.

Possibly the first step in the now luxuriant "Calasso legend" had its origin in a phrase uttered by the founder of the Frankfurt School, Theodor Adorno. After meeting a very young Calasso, Adorno commented: "This Roberto has not only read all the books I've written, but also those I've yet to write." This is recorded in the annals of publishing.

Translated from the Spanish by Gabriel Abramowicz

EDWIN FRANK

FOR ROBERTO

Once upon a time I was a student of art history living for some months in Rome and doing research toward a PhD. Research meant going to churches to see the dark pictures that interested me, and since it was fall and the days were also growing dark I did this in the morning, when there was a chance of at least some natural illumination. I liked poking around churches and chapels and looking at pictures, but the more I did, the less it seemed there was for me to write about them, or not, in any case, in the way I was expected to. So in the afternoon rather than writing I read—Boswell's *Life of Johnson*, which did fill up the hours—and when I was tired of reading, I simply walked. It was on one of those walks that I went in to a bookstore and discovered Adelphi Edizioni, the books with their simultaneously severe and sumptuous jackets all set apart in a separate corner of their own, the shelves loaded with authors and titles of which some were familiar to me and much beloved while many others were not, though they seemed rich and strange: *Il Regno Segreto*; *Tesi per la fine del problema di Dio*. That one in fact I couldn't resist buying, if only, it may be, because the title hid a promise that God might put an end to the problem of my thesis.

And as it happened, a few years later, providentially, that problem did go away. Quite unexpectedly, I found myself involved in a publishing venture. Rea Hederman, the publisher of the *New York Review of Books*, asked me to put together a series of books that for one reason or another had been neglected in English—this became the NYRB Classics series—and as I took up the task Adelphi came to mind. That was what I'd like to put together, a list of books that, like Adelphi's, had a character of its own, mercurial but unmistakable, and that served as a clue to the great labyrinth of the world's thought and literature, a list in which losing and finding oneself would be, just as in reading a good book, one and the same thing. From the start, Adelphi was both inspiration and resource for NYRB, and now it has been almost twenty years that I have been doing my best to follow the extraordinary, inimitable, example that Roberto has set.

This morning, so many years after those mornings in Roman churches, I have been reading the wonderful fifth book of Wordsworth's *Prelude*, where he pays tribute to the stories we read in childhood, stories whose characters and images may in the dreary and dangerous stretches of life come back to protect and comfort us. At a low point in my own life Adelphi showed up, like—well, I'm reminded of the three figures of Long, Broad, and Sharpsight in a fairy tale that was one of my favorites as a child. (I read it in Robert Graves's *Book of Wizards*.) Long could cover any distance in a stride. Broad could encompass worlds. And Sharpsight could of course see everything everywhere. There you have it: Adelphi and Roberto in Hamlet's infinite nutshell. Here is what Wordsworth says:

> oh, then we feel, we feel,
> We know, when we have friends! Ye dreamers, then,
> Forgers of lawless tales, we bless you then,
> Impostors, drivellers, dotards, as the ape
> Philosophy will call you: then we feel
> With what, and how great might ye are in league,
> Who make our wish, our power, our thought a deed,
> An empire, a possession; ye whom time
> And seasons serve—all faculties—to whom
> Earth crouches, the elements are potter's clay,
> Space like a heaven filled up with northern lights,
> Here, nowhere, there, and everywhere at once.

Thank you, Roberto.

EVA BARBAROSSA

READING ADELPHI

It is November of 2015. I sit down with Roberto Calasso's small book, *The Art of the Publisher*. It is quite late when I begin, later than I am usually awake. I have carried this book all day, waiting for a moment when I can read it. Sleep is secondary tonight.

The first essay is the creation myth of the Adelphi publishing house. It is Calasso's vision of publishing as a form of art, a way of creating meaning. It tells of the ways in which this art spreads outward into the lives of readers, and into the intellectual life of a country. It begins in 1962, with the house, but also thousands of years before, with the creation of the first books Adelphi chooses to publish.

Calasso tells us of his vision of the art of publishing in which each book of a house is a chapter in a larger book. I can't help but wonder, what is this Book? What story is he telling? As I read on, more questions surface, swirl, dissipate.

I want to know more, but it is impossible to know, without at least looking at all the chapter headings, by which I mean: each book title. The selection of authors and the order of publication are an act of intent, and thus, of art.

The book of Adelphi, if you wish to read it in its entirety, requires the reading of parts. I read this small book. I make markings in the margins. I end with more questions, no answers, but an idea of where I might begin. I must begin with the parts.

•

I became acquainted with the writings of Roberto Calasso in my twenties. I had just graduated with a degree in languages and culture and was living in

San Francisco. It was the early '90s and SF was still rough around the edges, a bit broken down, still open for all possibilities, not yet the shiny tech city of the 2000s. There was a lot of space to be whomever you wanted to be, but not a lot of work, and not a lot of money. My degree, while interesting, wasn't clearly useful, and so I held several jobs to stay afloat, slept little, availed myself of a world of artists and writers.

Around the corner from my tiny flat in the upper Haight was a small used bookstore. My decor consisted of a bed, and books, little more. Most days I would wander in the shop, at least to see, usually not to buy. Sometimes it was enough to run my fingers along spines, open the old books, to inhale, to read a small passage. I saved my money, scrimping, for books, always more books.

There was one young man who worked there, Ruben. He was slim and quiet, wearing glasses as the cliché dictates. He would hold back books for me. When I entered he would reach under the counter to hand me my prize. He was very good. Most were books I had not yet read. Most were books I wanted to read but did not yet know of.

Back then I was reading as many mystical, magical, and ancient books that I could find. I was re-absorbing Latin and Greek classics, and re-addressing a great deal of philosophy, particularly those books which made me angry. It was in this particular shop that I first came upon the Eridanos Library. The first of the Library which I read was Pierre Klossowski's novel, *The Baphomet*. Eridanos' books were beautifully designed, the textures, the colors, the cover design, the paper, the font, the fold over flaps. They were visual and tactile. They brought pleasure before they were opened. It was the first publishing house whose books really struck me as works of art themselves, before even getting to the words. I would later learn that they too had their eye on Adelphi.

Their catalog was also notable. They were publishing Robert Musil, Ernst Jünger, Alberto Savino, Michel Leiris, Alexander Lernet-Holenia, Gesualdo Bufalino, Raymond Radiguet, Tommaso Landolfi, Cesare Pavese. Books I hadn't seen in print except in a library, and rarely in English. Eridanos seemed special, foreign, aware, in an older way, in a way that I was not born into.

Without registering the intent, I began to collect their books when I could find them. It didn't matter if I knew the author's name or anything about his work, being published by Eridanos was enough. I collected the small stack in my window, so I could look up and see the beautiful spines at any moment. These new authors opened new worlds, a Europe I had not yet experienced or seen.

It was a time of expansion in to new spaces, new lands, new literatures, and also a time in which I was seeking elusive answers to vaguely formed questions. Answers I thought that literature and philosophy could bring to me.

•

One afternoon when I popped into the bookstore the book which came out from beneath the desk was Roberto Calasso's *The Ruin of Kasch*. I had never heard of the author, but Ruben had a good track record, and so I took it with me, around the corner, and into bed, the only furniture in my flat on which to read.

I consumed it. I stayed up all night reading. It fit well with what was in my head, my undergraduate education had been half in French. I was full of the history and the literature, as well as mythology, the classics and philosophy. I had never read a book quite like it. *The Ruin of Kasch* rewove history into shapes and forms I had yet to experience. I was in a dream state, a haze. I sat and read from beginning to end. It was a revelation of how one could intertwine fiction and non-fiction, history and mythology, how a book could tear apart the categories and structures of knowledge and rebuild them into new worlds. I, too, began to retell the histories I knew, weaving and re-weaving outside the boundaries.

•

It was also at this time I began to attentively take notes on every book I read. I kept them only in a particular style of chemistry notebook, gray-blue with yellow, numbered pages, which I would find on sale at the ends of school years, and buy by the tens, if not more.

Each book I read was entered in the order in which it was read. No other organizing principle. I wrote only on the right-hand page. The left side was for notes, or reconsiderations, as well as connections to books I would read later. In the backs of the notebooks I collected lists of words and concepts, as well as bits and pieces of languages. These notebooks became a collection of the history of my thought, my education, of my learning to weave.

In these years I read with a certain type of starvation. I had an intensified desire, a need for there to be some outcome that would allow me to put the books down, lift my head, and understand something about life. This never happened, of course. Three, maybe four years into this, I did put down the books. Not with a sense of understanding anything more of life, but with a realization that there were no answers, no absolutes, no gods, and that it did not matter. And thus with no expectation of having answers, I returned to a more normal life, and stopped seeking. I still read, of course, but for pleasure.

Until the day I bought Calasso's *The Art of the Publisher* and found myself again tossed into the deep end.

•

I open my computer, pull up the Adelphi website, and I scrape every title and author for the 653 books in the Biblioteca Adelphi series. I dump them in a spreadsheet, so I can see them all in a single list. Will the titles tell me what this Book is?

No, they will not. Nor will the authors. Instead, the collection is so eclectic, so odd, so unusually ordered that I have only more questions. I am curious, perhaps obsessively curious, as to what Calasso is trying to tell the world in the creation of this catalog.

So I continue on. I add more information. I translate the titles and authors into English and French. I put in the original publication date of each book. I have more information, but no more insight. What do I see? I know it is not chaos. I can see no obvious rhyme or reason, no quickly visible pattern or sense that pops to the forefront. But I have just next to me this little book which tells me there is reason, there is sense, there is some bigger message in the collection and order of books chosen.

Of the Biblioteca Adelphi books, I had read about a third. None of them in Italian. Not enough to fill in the gaps or to make leaps of intuition. I cannot safely make any assumptions. Of the first ten Adelphi published, I have read only two and these, decades past. The only way I can see to go forward is to read.

I order the first four books, those published in 1965. Alfred Kubin, Edmund Gosse, Jan Potocki, René Daumal. Original years of publication: 1908, 1907, 1847, 1937. Austrian, English, Polish, French. Genres: science fiction, autobiography, a phantasmagoric tale, fiction. What can this mean?

Each book raises its own questions: Why this book? What was the author thinking? Calasso has written that it is not just the book, but also the order of the books, which matter. Why Kubin then Gosse? Why Gosse then Potocki? How do these fit together? Are these pieces of a puzzle? Do they interlock? Are they speaking to each other?

For the next several days I fill in more information on the books. The original publication languages (thirty-seven), birth and death locations and dates of each author, main cities lived in, I go on and on, lost in a haze of data, unable to see meaning. While there is no obvious pattern to understand the larger questions, patterns begin to surface. Clusters around Vienna, connections between authors, the spread of migrations and travel by countries and cities.

Complexities arise from the beginning: What nationality is a person born into a country which no longer exists when he writes his book? How does one classify a Hungarian born in Austria who writes in French? What becomes of the identity of an author in exile, who is he? In order to look for patterns,

I need to classify the items, but there are no sharp edges. How do I fill in the fields when they have more than one answer?

I order the next ten books on the list. I think I will only have to read a certain number of these books, and then I will see.

I continue to believe this for the first year.

•

Calasso and Roberto "Bobi" Bazlen seemed to share a vision. They believe in "i libri unici," singular books. Both Calasso and Bazlen ask the question, what trace is left of the experience of life? Calasso looks to the Vedas. There is no life without sacrifice and no sacrifice without residue; thus the book is the ash of experience. As for the singularity, in *The Art of Publishing* he writes, it is the book " . . . in which it is clear that something has happened to the author and has been put into writing," writes Calasso. The book must exist, so that we can remember what happened.

Each book I read brings me more questions—about the author, the book, their life. If Calasso is correct, that this is residue, I want to know what happened in the lives of each author to necessitate their writing this book. With each book I read, I long to read the next.

The more I read the less I know, the more my fascination grows, and thus a plan is hatched: I will read all 653 books in the same order in which Calasso and Adelphi chose to publish them. I will see, if I follow in the steps of the authors as well as in the steps of Calasso, if I can begin to see the shape of this book of Adelphi.

I order more books. They begin to stack up. On the tables, and the chairs, the desk, then the floor. Soon, even the counters and the stove have stacks, and I eat only cold foods. I find more questions, and I begin to ask these questions to others, as well as to myself.

•

These are books about religion, mysticism, seeking, philosophy. Many are books I read before, when I decided that there were no answers, so reading and seeking had no value. I feel as though I am about to begin again, but in a new way. When I review the catalog I imagine, in the future, one day, I will have to question everything I believe in, or, at least, I must question this comfortable place I stopped in. I sense that it will begin again, these questions, about me, about the world, about life, and the larger questions, those of meaning and purpose. I find myself looking forward to this, this reinvestigation of meaning, through the eyes of others and thus through my eyes. But I also think that this will take a while.

It takes four weeks.

I begin to ask my friends about god over tea, about the meaning of life over wine. I ask about family, and travel, dreams and psychology. I begin to ask strangers their opinions as well. The conversation we turn over and around is about spirituality. How can you believe in spirituality but not god? What is magic if not god? What does it mean to trust in the unseen? What does it mean to believe? Nothing about this goes as planned. Was there a plan? What is the difference between the sacred and the secular? My life changes faster than I thought it would.

I think of René Daumal in book number 19, *Mount Analogue*. "You cannot stay on the summit forever; you have to come down again. So why bother in the first place? Just this: What is above knows what is below, but what is below does not know what is above. One climbs, one sees. One descends, one sees no longer, but one has seen. There is an art of conducting oneself in the lower regions by the memory of what one saw higher up. When one can no longer see, one can at least still know." I climb, this time, I want to see differently.

•

I begin at the beginning. I read Arthur Kubin's *The Other Side*, Biblioteca Adelphi number 1. It is a phantasmagoric tale, dystopian, and leaves me with a sense of damaged lives and unrelenting loss. It is a story of a man invited to visit a city created in central Asia, by a former schoolmate in a Dream Realm. "The Dream Realm," Kubin writes "is a sanctuary for all those who are unhappy with modern civilization and contains everything necessary to cater for their bodily needs," and then it descends into surrealism and horror.

It is not obvious to me why Biblioteca Adelphi chose to publish it first. So I read more about Kubin and his world. Kubin was an Austrian, who wrote his book in 1908. It is described that he fell into a three-month delirium, composed this novel, and upon completing it was committed to an asylum. He does later return to illustration and never writes another book. He lived most of his life in a remote castle, after failing to commit suicide on his mother's grave. He was friends with Kafka, Klee, and Kandinsky, among others.

What is it about that place, that time, that made this book possible. How can I understand unless I can be there? I wish to be contemporary with this author, to "fling myself," as Roland Barthes puts it, "into the illusion that I am contemporary."

I opt to read Kubin in English and I order the book from the internet. I discover, after I've read it, that the translation I read had cut from it eighty pages an earlier translation. Eighty pages at the end in which Kubin updates the book with each reprinting, with notes on the world, himself, what has changed. When I finally find an old used copy of that version—remaindered from the National Library of Scotland, it is a moment of epiphany, the importance of version, of translation. This will vex me throughout the project.

I spend, in the early days, the first six months or so, a certain amount of time refreshing my memory of history. I begin to be immersed in the past, and find I must reweave, it is neither linear, nor a point. History books are written in chunks: Hungary, Modernism, the Weimar Republic. I need these to be one, to lay the tapestry beneath my exploration, and so I must recreate a view of history as I work, an interwoven model that suits the method by which I am seeking.

Book one results in my reading five additional books. Book two adds three more. Book three, an additional three. With this kind of math, the project will not take the three years I envisioned when I began, but four or five, possibly forever. I constantly feel as though I don't understand, or don't understand *enough*. In the early days, there was a lot to learn.

•

It becomes clearer as I work that the questions matter far more than the answers. This is a form of mutable self-consideration. There will never be just one answer to each question. Better to locate and gather the best questions, not the best answers, and ask them of myself over and over. Somehow, someday, this may all come together, into a vision, not only of Adelphi, but of the world, of meaning, of me. It all starts with questions, and with desire, and, of course, with life.

The experiences of these authors, they are the moments in which *they* do not know, the moments in which they want to know, the moments in which they cry out. It is their unwritten questions, the deep structures of their experience, the desires that drove them to write the book, this is what I seek.

I begin to collect their cries in my notebooks, their questions. They fill pages after page.

> "In the almost film-like flitting-by of modern life, a man needs something to tell him, from time to time, that he is still himself." Konrad Lorenz, *King Solomon's Ring*

> "There is inside me something horrible which rises and which does not come from me, but from the shadows that I have in me, where the soul of man does not know where the *I* begins and where it ends, or what made it begin as it sees itself." Antonin Artaud, *The Peyote Dance*

Their answers, and their lives, are compelling, fascinating. The friends they keep, the places they see, the epistolary exchanges. These are context to better expose their cries. I begin to collect their histories, as well, their friends, their habits. I draw maps, and then I move on.

It seems that what I am seeking is the opposite of a grand unifying theory. I do not want all the answers, I still do not believe in answers, but what I want is to belong—to myself, to this world, to a tradition—and these books, in their collection and their order, are teachers and guides. I have a long way to go, we shall see.

These books are my guides, as is Calasso and his vision for Adelphi. Perhaps all literature, all writing, all stories, are part of a way of being human, and this attentively created collection is a most capable map to understanding the nature of myself, and the world. I find myself on a path before I realize there is one.

·

These books mix and fuse. I imagine them in conversation with each other, and also with me. I read them in order, but my mind seeks other views, new patterns, groupings, and collections. By country, by nationality, by language, by time period, by city, even. By genre, by theme.

I draw a chalk map of 1938 Europe on the floor of my studio, and I take the books off the shelf and I stack them by country of origin. But the map is wrong. I move the books to the side, and wash the floor, and redraw the map. 1913 Europe. I restack the books. This seems better, but there are still problems.

When I begin my work each morning I look at the map and the stacks. And at the edges of my map, where I have stacks of books that do not belong to this map, from the countries not represented, or authors for whom I cannot choose a country. The stacks are a topography which speaks but which I cannot yet understand.

The Adelphi site offers me a page to sort their literature by theme, though they aren't the same themes I want, but I still explore. I have an affinity for boats and being at sea; tell me which books go to sea. What does it matter? Is there something that comes from putting to water? Jason and the Argonauts, Odysseus, even Charon, who crosses the water. Dante. Here I have *Moby-Dick, Treasure Island, The Island of the Colorblind.* Are islands the same as being at sea? It is certainly implied, that water was crossed. Shiel's *The Purple Cloud.* There are books written by authors who live on islands. *Omeros, White Egrets.*

I have questions and I will always have more. It is where I start.

I repaint an entire wall of my studio with chalkboard paint to give myself space to think out loud. I think in maps. Geographies, network maps, social graphs—everyone knew everyone, it seems. I also make lists, so I can look at them, ponder their structures or interactions of data. One day I list every Russian author in the catalog in order by birth date. Then I add all the major Russian authors who are not in the catalog. A few days later I add a timeline of history against which to think about these authors. A few months later I list all of the books of Vedic origin, then all those authors whose books contained Vedic concepts. A few days later I start to map the ideas, to see if I can understand the flow of these concepts through the literature itself. (I don't finish that one to my satisfaction. I will have to do it again, another day.) The wall changes week by week, depending on what I am pondering. I collect photos of the walls, as moments in time, erase, and begin again.

•

Something else is happening in my mind.

Calasso spoke of these books as chapters in the book of Adelphi, but I have a different image. It is an image of Calasso, at his desk—that iconic photo, but with a box on the floor next to him, an old cardboard box, bent edges, dusty, decades old. Within this box are the stone tesserae used to build a mosaic, cubes of color. He reaches into the box, picks out a stone, rotates it to find the perfect facet of this perfectly chosen stone, and places it in the sky, in the form of a constellation.

I envision Calasso creating a constellation, weaving meaning into the sky, built from the glittering and winky tesserae, a mosaic of books which, even once I could envision the shape of his constellation, I would still need the myth, the story, of what this creature was and why it was in the sky. His constellation is his map. What better place to put your map than where it can be seen? His map cannot be mine, I am my own cartographer, but I am curious to see what happens if I navigate to his map.

This is a linear creation story with a nonlinear output. Following the path does not give me each incremental step in the story, because the steps were not formatted that way, they are gathered from across time and culture. They are linear only in the moment, and then they fragment, into their pieces, the formation of meaning shifting and changing with each individual view. But to see Calasso's view I must gather his pieces and see what I see.

So I will follow the linear to the nonlinear, the individual to the collective. I shall walk a path, looking down, making sure the proper steps are taken so that I can look up, to the sky, to the night, and watch the mythos written out by these stars. And with this, I shall begin to build my own map, my own constellation, and then I shall find my own stones, and I shall find my own night sky.

•

These questions, this curiosity, began, quietly, in my apartment. I order and stack up books on all the surfaces. I read fiendishly in the mornings. I mention my project to a few friends. They are, in my estimation, surprisingly interested. First by the enormity of the project. They call it insane. Then they too are caught up in the conversations, the themes, the questions. They do not want to walk this path, read these books, but they want to watch. Voyeurs to my discovery, my struggle. As I work, the scope expands.

The was never meant to be exhaustive, or systematic. I just wander in any direction that raises up. The culs-de-sac are often as interesting as this central line. What I seek is a map, a wayfinding system. Cairns on the road, stars in a sky. I look for my own path, my own meaning, in the residue of others.

The only straight line that exists is the numerical order of the books as published by Adelphi. The choices of books, and the order they published them in is a hopscotch of dates, times, countries, periods, genres. There is no obvious rhyme or reason, which is how I've ended up here in this project, in the first place.

Humans seek patterns, humans tell stories. Two traits we have long recognized. We seek patterns even when they do not exist, we find meaning where meaning was not left for us, this is part of what it means to be human. By which I mean: we create patterns, we fabricate meaning. We tell stories because it is the way we turn straight lines into complex shapes. We make tales that have paths, we create ways to navigation, be they by the stars or by maps or by songs etched beneath the surface of the planet.

·

In parallel to the books, I read about the worlds in which the books came to be. Early twentieth-century Austria, the Habsburg Empire, religious cults in England, the Tarahumara Indians, the rise of modernism, 1968, brutalist architecture, the Spanish flu epidemic of 1917, Viennese cafe culture, psychoanalysis. I could go on. I read whatever seems to be the required to understand the authors, to become a local, of sorts.

I am reading books in five languages and I begin to run into trouble with the translations. I do not read German or Russian. The translations, and the editions, are difficult to choose. Opinions about translators are strong, and often opposing.

In an attempt to better understand Calasso I go back to the Sanskrit texts, the Rg Veda, the origin of his concept of residue, and his explanation for the creation of these books by their authors. The text that he cites as the source of how he evaluates each text for publication and also the texts that are woven through his work, *Ardor* and *Ka*. Within the Vedas, the Upanishads, I seek a greater understanding of the core mythology of the creation of Adelphi.

I create five pathways of exploration. I write them on a piece of paper and stick it to the barren yellow wall above my desk. The first is to read the Biblioteca Adelphi in order. The second is to reread all of Calasso's books in order. I had read him over decades, I want to read him all at once. The third is to explore the history of anything related to any of these books. The fourth is to reread the Vedas. The fifth, to read the history of twenty-century Italy. Later, I add a sixth: to read the history of other publishing houses with notable publishers: The Aldine Press, Minuit, Suhrkamp, and Pantheon.

•

Most of these books that Calasso published in Italian I am reading in English or French. Some of the Italians I read in Italian. I wonder what they sounded like in their original languages, these books. There are thirty-seven original languages on the list, counting German only once, which is probably not proper, given the varieties.

There is the concept of sound, of resonance, of the meaning entailed in sound, of the sacred. Of the meanings that come from the sounds themselves, not the words. Without the proper pronunciation the secret power cannot be unlocked. I think of Hinduism and the *bija* sounds, of the sound that creates the world. If you mispronounce the sound, no world will be created. And a mantra must be pronounced aloud to work. Sound requires vibration to transmit its magic.

I read the books aloud, to my room, to my chalkboard wall, in one language or another, with an eye at the ready to glimpse some change take place in my peripheral vision. I don't believe they have the proper meaning when read aloud in translation.

Will there be a primeval resonance that creates its own meaning? Are these forms of music? Is meaning encoded in the sound, not the word? Many of these books began as oral forms. What was lost in writing? And in translation? I cannot know this, and, despite the desire, I doubt I can learn thirty-seven languages and their unique cultures to a degree that I could read all of these books in their original languages. I find this compelling, however. How many languages can Calasso read? Many, I know. A classical education, a European, a self-taught Sanskrit scholar.

Each answer I find is ephemeral. The next answer may be as right as this one.

I move between microscope and telescope. I slip between time. I become all the sounds of language. I know nothing. I am exactly where I want to be. I start over, from my youth, at the beginning, a beginning, and find the beginning is in the middle, and even if I wanted to, I could not locate the beginning or the end.

•

A year into my project I write an essay and put it on the internet, "Reading the Catalog," and I find myself with followers, admirers, and Italian-language press. One note I received was from Calasso, and we forge a connection of sorts. He begins to send me copies of the books, in Italian. I discover it is not just the sound of the texts as they were in their original languages that I am missing. There are two things specific to the Biblioteca editions themselves. The cover images, which Calasso writes of in his essay—of the difficulty in finding the image that speaks to a person who has not read the book and still again after they have. The book blurbs, rumored to be written by Calasso, which bring to mind the introductory letters Aldus Manutius wrote for the Greek texts he published. Are the blurbs plus the images Calasso's introductory letters? And in them are there hints to what he is telling us in the book of Adelphi? As I have only some of the books, I cannot look at them all. I imagine laying the entire series out on the floor of my studio, hundreds of beautifully designed books, with purposefully chosen covers, in their subtle design. What story would I see with these visuals? Are they, too, a story of their own? I think so, but I still do not know.

•

To follow this path, I must accept relativity—of knowledge, of language, of translation, of belief. I can believe anything I want, but it will only be my belief. The answers I have chosen to be correct may only be my choice. I find this to be a form of freedom. I find, again, that the answers do not matter, even if I have them. The questions matter, and with these books, I can ask them again and again.

The further I read, the more similarities I see, however, in what is being sought, in how it is being sought, and in what is being found. It could be the curation, it could be the authors, or it could be that they are all on to something. I do not know, and in my way, I do not care, I keep going—reading, questioning, exploring.

Seven hundred books written over 2700 years. Two hundred and eighty-five authors.

•

I look for myself in all these stories, in all the authors. I can't help it. In the attempt to be present at their moment of singularity I attempt to exist as them, to inhabit their selves, their thoughts and ideals. To listen to the world as it is at the moment when their books were born. With these questions, with these books, I simply take the next step, I read, I think, I map.

Sometimes I do return to the most basic of questions: Why does it matter? Why did this matter to Calasso? What world was Adelphi building, in Italy, with these books? What particular path do these books, alone and together, describe? If I walk it, what will I see?

I will place my glittering stones into the sky knowing full well that my constellation will never be his constellation. Let us see what I find. What will be the shape of the way I find to travel?

A ROBERTO CALASSO READING LIST

THE WORK IN PROGRESS

La rovina di Kasch. Milan: Adelphi Edizioni, 1983. [*The Ruin of Kasch*, translated by Richard Dixon. New York: Penguin, 2018.]

Le nozze di Cadmo e Armonia. Milan: Adelphi Edizioni, 1988. [*The Marriage of Cadmus and Harmony*, translated by Tim Parks. New York: Knopf, 1993.]

Ka. Milan: Adelphi Edizioni, 1996. [*Ka*, translated by Tim Parks. New York: Knopf, 1998.]

K. Milan: Adelphi Edizioni, 2002. [*K.*, translated by Geoffrey Brock. New York: Knopf, 2005.]

Il rosa Tiepolo. Milan: Adelphi Edizioni, 2006. [*Tiepolo Rose*, translated by Alastair McEwen. New York: Knopf, 2009]

La Folie Baudelaire. Milan: Adelphi Edizioni, 2008. [*La Folie Baudelaire*, translated by Alastair McEwen. New York: Knopf, 2012.]

L'ardore. Milan: Adelphi Edizioni, 2010. [*Ardor*, translated by Richard Dixon. London: Penguin Books, 2014.]

Il Cacciatore Celeste. Milan: Adelphi Edizioni, 2016. [*The Celestial Hunter*, forthcoming from Penguin and FSG in a translation by Richard Dixon.]

L'innominabile attuale. Milan: Adelphi Edizioni, 2017. [*The Unnamable Present,* translated by Richard Dixon. New York: Farrar Straus Giroux, *2019*]

OTHER WORKS

L'impuro folle. Milan: Adelphi Edizioni, 1974.

I quarantanove gradini. Milan: Adelphi Edizioni, 1991. [*The Forty-Nine Steps*, translated by John Shepley. Minneapolis: University of Minnesota Press, 2001.]

La letteratura e gli dèi. Milan: Adelphi Edizioni, 2001. [*Literature and the Gods*, translated by Tim Parks. New York: Knopf, 2001.]

Cento lettere a uno sconosciuto. Milan: Adelphi Edizioni, 2003.

La follia che viene dalle Ninfe. Milan: Adelphi Edizioni, 2005.

L'impronta dell'editore. Milan: Adelphi Edizioni, 2013. [*The Art of the Publisher*, translated by Richard Dixon. New York: Farrar Straus Giroux, 2015.]

CONTRIBUTORS

Alex Andriesse is the translator of Chateaubriand's *Memoirs from Beyond the Grave*, published by NYRB Classics, and of Roberto Bazlen's *Notes without a Text and Other Writings*, published by Dalkey Archive Press.

Luis Alberto Ayala Blanco, born in Mexico City in 1969, is the author of the book-length essay *El silencio de los dioses* (2004), *Autómatas espermáticos* (2005), and a volume of aphorisms, *99* (2009). He completed his degree in Political Science at the Universidad Nacional Autónoma de México, where he taught political philosophy for more than a decade, with a thesis on the work of Roberto Calasso.

John Banville was born in Wexford, Ireland in 1945. He is the author of many novels, including *The Book of Evidence*, *The Sea* (winner of the Man Booker Prize), and *Mrs. Osmond*.

Eva K. Barbarossa is a writer, traveler, and independent scholar.

Joseph Brodsky (1940–1996) was born in Leningrad and came to the United States in 1972 as an involuntary exile from the Soviet Union. The author of many books of poetry and prose, he received the Nobel Prize in Literature in 1987 and in 1991 was appointed Poet Laureate of the United States.

Italo Calvino (1923–1985) is one of the major Italian writers of the twentieth century. He is the author of the novels *The Baron in the Trees*, *Invisible Cities*, and *If on a Winter's Night a Traveler*, in addition to many other works.

Pietro Citati, born in Florence in 1930, has written biographies of such figures as Goethe, Tolstoy, Kafka, Katherine Mansfield, and Proust; a memoir of his friendship with Italo Calvino; and many other books of essays and scholarship.

Wendy Doniger is the Mircea Eliade Distinguished Service Professor of the History of Religions at the University of Chicago. She is the author of over forty books, including *The Hindus: An Alternative History*, *Hinduism* (in the Norton Anthology of World Religions), and *Against Dharma: Dissent in the Ancient Indian Sciences of Sex and Politics*.

Edwin Frank is the editorial director of NYRB Classics and the author of *Snake Train: Poems 1984–2013*.

Jorge Herralde is an award-winning editor, and the founder and director of Editorial Anagrama.

Andrea Lee is the author of *Russian Journal*, *Sarah Phillips*, *Interesting Women: Stories*, and *Lost Hearts in Italy: A Novel*.

Charles Malamoud, born in 1929, is a historian of religions and Indologist. He is the author of many articles and books on the history of India and on Vedic thought, including *Le Jumeau Solitaire* (The Solitary Twin, 2002), *La Danse des pierres* (The Dance of the Stones, 2005), and *Cooking the World: Ritual and Thought in Ancient India* (Oxford University Press, 1996).

Francisco Rico is Professor of Medieval Hispanic Literature at the Universidad Autónoma de Barcelona and a member of the Royal Spanish Academy. He directs the History and Criticism of Spanish Literature series as well as the Classical Library published by Editorial Critica. He has edited critical editions of *Don Quixote* and *Lazarillo de Tormes* and is the author of *The Spanish Picaresque Novel and the Point of View* (published by Cambridge University Press, 1984), *Tiempos del "Quijote"* (Times of *Don Quixote*, 2012), and *El sueño del humanismo* (The Dream of Humanism, 1993), which has been translated into French, Italian, and Japanese.

Elena Sbrojavacca received her doctorate from the Università Ca'Foscari Venezia. Her dissertation, "Roberto Calasso o della Letteratura Assoluta" (2018), addresses Calasso's conception of Absolute Literature.

Charles Simic is the author of more than twenty books of poetry, in addition to essays and memoirs. He is the recipient of the Pulitzer Prize, the Griffin Prize, the MacArthur Fellowship, and the Wallace Stevens Award. He has also been Poet Laureate of the United States.

The Antioch Review

http://review.antiochcollege.org

Publishing prominent and promising poets & authors for over 75 years

A. Leon Higginbotham, Aimee Bender, Allen Ginsberg, Cate Marvin, Elaine Showalter, Jorie Graham, Joyce Carol Oates, Leon Panetta, Rod Serling, Robert K. Merton, Sylvia Plath, Henry Louis Gates, Jr., Harryette Mullen, W. S. Merwin, Cynthia Ozick, Norman Thomas di Giovanni, Jamie Quatro, Gordon Lish, Lily Tuck, T. Coraghessan Boyle, Lewis Corey, Ralph Ellison, Gerald Early, Clifford Geertz . . . and more.

Purchase online: http://review.antiochcollege.org/store

Mail Order: For the **two-issue set** send $25.00 US, $40.00 Canada, $50.00 International with check or money order payable to *Antioch Review*, P. O. Box 148, Yellow Springs, OH 45387. **Single issue Part I:** $12.50 US, $23.00 Canada, $33.00 International; **Single issue Part II:** $25.00 US, $40.00 Canada, $45.00 International $50.00.

PUERTO DEL SOL

www.puertodelsol.org

"Long before the San Francisco Renaissance exploded with public and police clamor and articles in Time, *Orlovitz was writing with a Dionysian frenzy combined with perfect control of language that has been equaled by few, if any, of the Beats."*
— Chad Walsh, *Today's Poets* (1964)

Compiled
and edited by
Rick Schober

Published by
Tough Poets Press
www.toughpoets.com

Publication date:
June 7, 2018

Format:
Papaerback,
274 pages,
5.8" x 8.3"

Retail price:
$15.99

GIL ORLOVITZ
What Are They All Waiting For?
Stories, Poems & Essays (1944-1962)

An anthology of long out-of-print works by one of America's most innovative, yet virtually forgotten, writers of the 20th century.

THE REVIEW OF CONTEMPORARY FICTION
BACK ISSUES AVAILABLE

Back issues are still available for the following numbers of the
Review of Contemporary Fiction ($8 each unless otherwise noted):

William Eastlake / Aidan Higgins

William S. Burroughs ($15)

Camilo José Cela

Chandler Brossard

Samuel Beckett

Claude Ollier / Carlos Fuentes

Joseph McElroy

John Barth / David Markson

Donald Barthelme / Toby Olson

William H. Gass / Manuel Puig

Robert Walser

José Donoso / Jerome Charyn

William T. Vollmann / Susan Daitch / David Foster Wallace ($15)

Angela Carter / Tadeusz Konwicki

Stanley Elkin / Alasdair Gray

Brigid Brophy / Robert Creeley / Osman Lins

Edmund White / Samuel R. Delany

Mario Vargas Llosa / Josef Škvorecký

Wilson Harris / Alan Burns

Raymond Queneau / Carole Maso

Curtis White / Milorad Pavi

Richard Powers / Rikki Ducornet

Edward Sanders

Writers on Writing: The Best of The *Review of Contemporary Fiction*

Bradford Morrow

Jean Rhys / John Hawkes / Paul Bowles / Marguerite Young

Henry Green / James Kelman / Ariel Dorfman

David Antin

Janice Galloway / Thomas Bernhard / Robert Steiner / Elizabeth Bowen

Gilbert Sorrentino / William Gaddis / Mary Caponegro / Margery Latimer

Italo Calvino / Ursule Molinaro / B. S. Johnson

Louis Zukofsky / Nicholas Mosley / Coleman Dowell

Casebook Study of Gilbert Sorrentino's *Imaginative Qualities of Actual Things*

Rick Moody / Ann Quin / Silas Flannery

Diane Williams / Aidan Higgins / Patricia Eakins

Douglas Glover / Blaise Cendrars / Severo Sarduy

Robert Creeley / Louis-Ferdinand Céline / Janet Frame

William H. Gass

Gert Jonke / Kazuo Ishiguro / Emily Holmes Coleman

William H. Gass / Robert Lowry / Ross Feld

Flann O'Brien / Guy Davenport / Aldous Huxley

Steven Millhauser

William Eastlake / Julieta Campos / Jane Bowles

Novelist as Critic: Essays by Garrett, Barth, Sorrentino, Wallace, Ollier, Brooke-Rose, Creeley, Mathews, Kelly, Abbott, West, McCourt, McGonigle, & McCarthy

New Finnish Fiction: Fiction by Eskelinen, Jäntti, Kontio, Krohn, Paltto, Sairanen, Selo, Siekkinen, Sund, & Valkeapää

New Italian Fiction: Interviews and fiction by Malerba, Tabucchi, Zanotto, Ferrucci, Busi, Corti, Rasy, Cherchi, Balduino, Ceresa, Capriolo, Carrera, Valesio, & Gramigna

Grove Press Number: Contributions by Allen, Beckett, Corso, Ferlinghetti, Jordan, McClure, Rechy, Rosset, Selby, Sorrentino, & others

New Danish Fiction: Fiction by Brøgger, Høeg, Andersen, Grøndahl, Holst, Jensen, Thorup, Michael, Sibast, Ryum, Lynggaard, Grønfeldt, Willumsen, & Holm

New Latvian Fiction: Fiction by Ikstena, Bankovskis, Berelis, Kolmanis, Ziedonis, & others

The Future of Fiction: Essays by Birkerts, Caponegro, Franzen, Galloway, Maso, Morrow, Vollmann, White, & others ($15)

New Japanese Fiction: Interviews & fiction by Ohara, Shimada, Shono, Takahashi, Tsutsui, McCaffery, Gregory, Kotani, Tatsumi, Koshikawa, & others

New Cuban Fiction: Fiction by Ponte, Mejides, Aguilar, Bahr, Curbelo, Plasencia, Serova, & others

Special Fiction Issue: *JUAN EMAR*: Fiction & illustrations by Juan Emar, translated by Daniel Borzutzky

New Australian Fiction: Fiction by Murnane, Tsiolkas, Falconer, Wilding, Bird, Yu, & others

New Catalan Fiction: Fiction by Rodoreda, Espriu, Ibarz, Monsó, Serra, Moliner, Serés, & others

Writers on Writing: Essays by Gail Scott, William H. Gass, Gert Jonke, Nicholas Delbanco, & others

Georges Perec Issue: Essays by Perec, Harry Mathews, David Bellos, Marcel Bénabou, & others

Special Fiction Issue: *; OR THE WHALE*: Radically abridged *Moby-Dick*, edited by Damion Searls

Individuals receive a 10% discount on orders of one issue and a 20% discount on orders of two or more issues. To place an order, use the form on the last page of this issue.

Order Form

Individuals may use this form to subscribe to the *Review of Contemporary Fiction* or to order back issues of the *Review* and Dalkey Archive titles at a discount (see below for details).

Title	ISBN	Quantity	Price

Subtotal _____

Less Discount _____
(10% for one book, 20% for two or more books, and 25% for Scholarly titles advertised in this issue)
Subtotal _____

Plus Postage _____
(U.S. $3 + $1 per book; foreign $7 + $5 per book)

***1 Year Individual Subscription to the* Review** _____
($17 U.S.; $22.60 Canada; $32.60 all other countries)
Total _____

Mailing Address _____

_____

_____

_____

xxxii/1

Credit card payment ☐ Visa ☐Mastercard

Acct. # _____ Exp. date _____

Name on card _____ Phone # _____

Billing zip code _____

Please make checks (in U.S. dollars only) payable to *Dalkey Archive Press*.

mail this form to: Dalkey Archive Press,
6271 E 535 North Road, McLean, IL 61754